TERRORISM
& the Media

DILEMMAS FOR GOVERNMENT,

JOURNALISTS & THE PUBLIC

EDITED BY Yonah Alexander

AND Richard Latter

BRASSEY'S (US), INC.

Maxwell Macmillan Pergamon Publishing Corp.

Washington · New York · London · Oxford

Beijing · Frankfurt · São Paulo · Sydney · Tokyo · Toronto

U.S.A. (Editorial)	Brassey's (US), Inc. 8000 Westpark Drive, 1st Floor, McLean, Virginia 22102, U.S.A.
(Orders)	Attn: Order Dept., Macmillan Publishing Co., Front & Brown Streets, Riverside, N.J. 08075
U.K. (Editorial)	Brassey's (UK) Ltd. 50 Fetter Lane, London EC4A 1AA, England
(Orders)	Brassey's (UK) Ltd. Headington Hill Hall, Oxford OX3 OBW, England
PEOPLE'S REPUBLIC OF CHINA	Pergamon Press, Room 4037, Qianmen Hotel, Beijing, People's Republic of China
FEDERAL REPUBLIC OF GERMANY	Pergamon Press GmbH, Hammerweg 6, D-6242 Kronberg, Federal Republic of Germany
BRAZIL	Pergamon Editora Ltda, Rua Eça de Queiros, 346, CEP 04011, Paraiso, São Paulo, Brazil
AUSTRALIA	Brassey's Australia, P.O. Box 544, Potts Point, N.S.W. 2011, Australia
JAPAN	Pergamon Press, 5th Floor, Matsuoka Central Building, 1-7-1 Nishishinjuku, Shinjuku-ku, Tokyo 160, Japan
CANADA	Pergamon Press Canada, Suite No. 271, 253 College Street, Toronto, Ontario, Canada M5T 1R5

PRINTED IN THE UNITED STATES OF AMERICA

Library of Congress Cataloging-in-Publication Data

Terrorism & the media : dilemmas for government, journalists & the public / edited by Yonah Alexander and Richard Latter.
    p.   cm.—(Brassey's (US) terrorism library)
Includes bibliographical references.
ISBN 0-08-037442-5 :
1. Terrorism in mass media. 2. Terrorism. I. Alexander, Yonah. II. Latter, Richard, 1949– . III. Title: Terrorism and the media. IV. Series.
P96.T47T47 1990
302.23—dc20   89-70784
                                                                        CIP

British Library Cataloguing in Publication Data

Terrorism & the media : dilemmas for government, journalists & the public.
1. Terrorism. Reporting by news media.
I. Alexander, Yonah. II. Latter, Richard 1949–
070.44932242
ISBN 0-08-037442-5

PRINTED IN THE UNITED STATES OF AMERICA

£12·50

TERRORISM
& the Media

Other Volumes in Brassey's Terrorism Library

Alexander & Picard   IN THE CAMERA'S EYE: NEWS COVERAGE OF
TERRORIST EVENTS

Hanle   TERRORISM: THE NEWEST FACE OF WARFARE

Other Titles of Related Interest

Charters & Tugwell   ARMIES IN LOW-INTENSITY CONFLICT

Leventhal & Alexander   NUCLEAR TERRORISM: DEFINING THE
THREAT

O'Neill   INSURGENCY & TERRORISM: INSIDE MODERN
REVOLUTIONARY WARFARE

Paschall   LIC 2010: SPECIAL OPERATIONS & UNCONVENTIONAL
WARFARE IN THE NEXT CENTURY

Taylor   THE TERRORIST

Related Journals*

Armed Forces Journal International

Defense Analysis

Survival

*Sample copies available upon request.

PUBLISHER'S NOTE

Brassey's Terrorism Library

THE MONOGRAPH SERIES

As terrorism continues as one of the most serious and lasting threats to the security of nations and to the safety of innocent citizens everywhere, the systematic and rational analysis of terrorism becomes even more important. Brassey's is thus publishing the Terrorism Library, a series of books designed to educate a concerned worldwide public. In order to provide the widest possible dissemination of information about terrorism, Brassey's will also publish monographs such as this one as part of the Terrorism Library. By disseminating these valuable monographs of terrorism-related collections, documents, papers, and studies, we hope to play some small part in the understanding of and response to terrorism.

CONTENTS

FOREWORD

Brassey's (US)
TERRORISM
Library

Terrorism, as a process of deliberate employment of psychological intimidation and physical violence by sovereign states and subnational groups to attain strategic and political objectives in violation of law, is not new in history. In modern times, along with the nuclear age, we are in the midst of the new "age of terrorism" with all its frightening consequences for the continuity of civilized order.

Indeed, terrorism has become a permanent fixture of contemporary life. It poses a variety of threats, including those related to the safety and welfare of ordinary people, the stability of the state system, the health and pace of economic development, and the expansion and even the survival of democracy. Today's terrorists are better organized, more professional, and better equipped than their historical counterparts. Technological developments offer new targets and new capabilities. Tomorrow's terrorists might resort to chemical, biological, or nuclear violence to achieve mass disruption or political turmoil.

In light of this likelihood, Brassey's (US), Inc., has developed its Terrorism Library. The purpose of this series is to offer books, written or edited by recognized experts, on a variety of subjects, including the causation and control of terrorism; national, regional, and global perspectives on terrorism; and specific case studies. Although each volume will stand on its own merit, the Terrorism Library will provide a comprehensive intellectual and professional framework for better understanding the nature, scope, intensity, and consequences of the threat of modern terrorism and what society can do to cope with this phenomenon in the 1990s.

PROFESSOR YONAH ALEXANDER
Series Editor

ix

PREFACE

Wilton Park was founded in 1946 as a forum for dialogue between Germans and Britons in an attempt to restore relations after the Second World War. Since then, Wilton Park has steadily broadened its range of conference topics and participating countries and by the 1980s it had become a global institution with participants from all parts of the world as well as from all the major professions. Security issues have always figured strongly in Wilton Park discussions, with numerous conferences on the NATO alliance, on arms control and disarmament, and on East-West relations.

During recent years, security conferences have become more optimistic. The "new thinking" in Soviet foreign policy, combined with the tough but flexible stance of the Western allies, created the conditions for a substantial warming of East-West relations. This change in turn is now leading to significant reductions in military personnel and equipment, together with a movement toward the resolution of conflicts in many of the world's trouble spots.

Unfortunately, these favorable developments in superpower and interbloc relations have not so far removed one major threat to security: the scourge of terrorism. Over the last twenty years, terrorism has flourished, and appears ineradicable despite the efforts of most of the world's governments and security forces to find effective countermeasures. Wilton Park has therefore devoted a number of conferences to the study of this problem.

Of the many dilemmas involved in countering terrorism, the relationship between the role of governments and security forces and that of the media is among the most agonizing for democratic societies. Without some restraints on the free dissemination of facts and opinion, the media can become an unwitting instrument in the terrorist cause. Yet if security against terrorism includes measures that destroy the credibility of the media, the terrorists will have won a great victory. The Wilton Park Conference on Terrorism and the Media held in January 1988 was devoted to the examination of these issues and resulted in interesting and significant conclusions.

These are set out in this volume as a further contribution by Wilton Park, in collaboration with the Institute for Studies in International Terrorism of the State University of New York, to international understanding.

GEOFFREY DENTON
Director of Wilton Park

Introduction

by Yonah Alexander and Richard Latter

THE THREAT posed by national and international terrorism has been much studied and debated in recent years. The consensus is that terrorism represents an identifiable threat to specific individuals, but the impact on society in general and the threat posed to the liberal democracies in particular remain subjects of contention. Walter Laqueur has noted, "There is a tendency to magnify the importance of terrorism in modern society: society is vulnerable to attack, but it is also astonishingly resilient. Terrorism makes a great noise, but so far it has not been very destructive."[1] In contrast, Paul Wilkinson observes that "internal terrorism constitutes a potentially grave problem for liberal democracy"[2] and that "terroristic ideology is inevitably and constantly deployed in a struggle to defame and discredit liberal democracy."[3] Whatever the long-term nature of the threat posed to society, terrorism undoubtedly has generated significant human suffering and economic damage and has altered patterns of human behavior, not least through the introduction of security arrangements on a global scale. However, the continued existence of numerous terrorist groups and their continuing capacity for action demonstrate that governments have been unable to cope effectively with the terrorist phenomenon.

A crucial area of debate has concerned the role of the media in reporting terrorist actions and, more generally, media ethics with regard to terrorism. The nature and levels of media coverage have come under critical scrutiny by security forces and governments and, to some degree, by the public. Although accepting the vital role of the press in maintaining a democratic society, many believe that "freedom of the press" must be exercised with caution and discretion in relation to terrorist incidents and campaigns. Inevitably, caution and discretion involve some curtailment of open reporting, whether effected by self-regulation or imposed through legislation. Restrictions on the media are opposed by those who believe unfettered reporting to be essential to the maintenance of democracy. How to maintain media freedom without offering inadvertent aid and comfort to terrorists remains an unresolved dilemma.

The Wilton Park Conference brought together groups within society most directly involved with the terrorism-and-the-media question: terrorism and counterterrorism experts (from government, the private sector, and aca-

1

demia); the victims of terrorist incidents (representing also, to a degree, the interested public); and representatives of the media. Following the contributions of these groups and discussion among them, the conference culminated in a simulation exercise in incident management that offered a vivid insight into the problems the media and others encounter when confronted with terrorist actions.

The substantive work of the conference was to study the impact of terrorism in democratic societies committed to freedom of the press. The views of government officials and academic experts regarding the proper role of the media in dealing with terrorist activity and the views of the press from three distinct media environments—the United States, the United Kingdom, and Western Europe—were examined. This introduction outlines the positions taken and closes with a summary of the areas of agreement and differences of opinion that emerged and of the conclusions drawn.

Whether terrorism is viewed primarily as an act of war or as a crime, the general consensus is that it involves the deliberate use or threat of violence, designed to create fear in a target population larger than the group of immediate victims, to achieve objectives in violation of the law. Reactions to terrorism, however, have been piecemeal and uncoordinated in the past, and Western governments have sometimes been slow to appreciate its consequences. The role of Western media in reporting terrorist events and government policies regarding media involvement reflect the lack of cohesion that has characterized reactions to terrorism in general. However, crucial issues for the media have been identified and are now under public debate. Major questions include the following:

1. Do news reports cause or encourage terrorism?
2. Would terrorism decline if the media ignored events?
3. Should media coverage of an event be delayed and in what circumstances?
4. Should attempts be made to deny reporters access to information?
5. Is it possible to legislate "legitimate" media coverage of incidents?
6. What should be the media's relationship with police?
7. Can the media take steps to minimize its exploitation by terrorists?
8. Is media self-censorship acceptable or possible, given competition between media agencies?
9. Should the media cover incidents in full?
10. Will media self-censorship lead terrorists to escalate violence to ensure that it is reported?

These questions derive from the assumptions that terrorism is essentially violence for effect (which is not to deny that bombings, for example, may be primarily designed to undermine the economy) and that publicity via the media is central to the success of the strategy. The quest of the media to secure news and to present events to attract an audience rather than to furnish information may result in an uncritical presentation of the terrorists' case. Although the media do not create terrorism, their actions may facilitate the strategic success of terrorist groups. Other negative effects include inciting the copying of actions published in the media by other groups, jeopardizing antiterrorist actions, and even direct involvement in incidents and unjustified participation in their management.

Others note that democracy can also be undermined by limitations on the freedom to disseminate information, thus achieving the terrorists' purpose. Evidence has been offered of governments using terrorist incidents or subsequent trials to bolster their own position or to increase their popularity during election campaigns. Release of hostages may be timed or negotiated with domestic political goals in mind. Boundaries must be established concerning the extent to which the public has a right to be informed and how far government and society may be prepared to go to curb this right. The right to know cannot be equated with the journalist's right to know and to report; journalists cannot make such a decision without being subject to the duly elected government. In some circumstances, the right to basic security overrides the right to know: acceptance of this proposition argues in favor of guidance or censorship by government in specified circumstances.

Reporting on terrorism may involve distinguishing between the existence of a legitimate cause and its promotion through illegitimate terrorist activity. For example, positive coverage of the Palestine Liberation Organization's aim to establish a Palestinian homeland and the African National Congress's goal of ending apartheid, two causes that have considerable international support, is to be coupled with rejection of terrorist methods. Opinions differ regarding the types and levels of violence that are acceptable in these circumstances. However, many reiterate the view that liberal democracies and the media must not confuse aims and means. Terrorism is to be rejected whatever the circumstances, and democracies are to support nonviolent opposition to repression.

Rejection of terrorism is also linked to evidence of its failure to promote its causes. The conflict in Northern Ireland, for example, grew out of a legitimate, peaceful civil rights movement. Although imperfect, means existed for grievances to be raised and pursued. The introduction of violence and related antidemocratic philosophies is said to have set back progress in the civil rights field and to have generated a polarization between Catholic and Protestant communities that lessened the possibility of constructive collaboration. Similar tensions exist throughout the world, most notably in Central America: confusion over the legitimacy of a cause and the use of terrorism is widespread. Liberal democracies have taken the view that, overall, international support for peaceful change represents the legitimate course of action. The media may act effectively to support this approach.

Problems of enacting this policy with international cooperation are evident, given the different interests of states involved. Concerted international action, including coordinated antiterrorist propaganda, offers a promising approach, particularly against state-sponsored terrorism; for example, evidence exists that Syrian involvement with terrorism has been reduced in the face of such pressure. Also, the shared values of government and media in liberal democracies can provide a basis on which to establish guidelines on reporting terrorism: the fundamental unacceptability of terrorism as a method, whatever the cause, is crucial.

New technologies provide terrorists with a means to promote their goals outside the mainstream media: pirate radio and TV stations, satellite TV, and underground newspapers. As the Western media forge a policy, however imperfect, regarding the reporting of terrorism, the terrorist will seek to exploit these new channels to optimize the propaganda effort. Given the psychology of terrorism and the related concern with propaganda, governments will be forced to continue to engage in the propaganda war. The psychological underpinnings of terrorist activity provide insights as to how this battle may be conducted successfully.

The debate over the role of the media and their coverage of terrorism demonstrates differences of opinion that are difficult to reconcile. However, areas of common ground do exist on which compromise and cooperation may be established between governments and media, given adequate understanding and respect for the other's views and concerns. The principal conclusions and issues are

1. Differences regarding the role media should play with regard to terrorism derive from differing perceptions of the level and nature of the threat terrorism poses to democracy, the varying responsibilities of different groups dealing with terrorism, and differing philosophical positions on the role of the media in a democratic society.

2. Terrorism may be viewed as a crime, occurring within otherwise peaceful societies, and is not to be considered an act of war. Terrorists are to be treated as criminals rather than as prisoners of war.

3. Both censorship and self-regulation are proposed by different groups as the only legitimate method of regulating media involvement with terrorism. Those who deal with terrorism directly tend to favor some form of government direction or censorship; the media generally favor self-regulation.

4. A balance is required between guaranteeing the public's right to security and its right to be informed. The freedom of the press to report is not, therefore, absolute.

5. Terrorism includes a significant propaganda dimension; the media should not assist terrorists in their effort to secure positive publicity.

6. Terrorists exhibit psychological traits that the authorities seek to exploit in incident resolution; media coverage should be consistent with and supportive of those efforts.

7. The media should act in a manner consistent with and supportive of the democratic system within which they function. Associated ethics

should be central to media coverage and override competitive or commercial factors.

8. The media have on occasion reported terrorism irresponsibly, and a negative attitude on the part of authorities dealing with incidents has resulted.

9. Irresponsible coverage may generate government action to restrict media freedoms.

10. The role played by the media differs in various countries because it is influenced by relevant legal provisions (the U.S. First Amendment, the U.K. Official Secrets Act), the structure of the media industry in a given country, and the nature of government-media relations derived from past experience with terrorist incidents.

11. In spite of differences, efforts to improve government-media cooperation, for the benefit of victims in particular, are occurring. Establishing a clear framework for cooperation, including respect for the independence and integrity of both parties, offers a positive method of resolving these contentious issues.

The Wilton Park Conference provided a forum where these issues were identified and debated by government and media representatives who were able to discuss in depth the views and perceptions of their respective professions. Although understanding may not be said to have led to complete agreement on every issue, all involved were able to identify clearly the points that separate and link them. Sufficient common ground was identified to provide a potential basis for a more positive relationship in the future.

NOTES

1. Walter Laqueur, "Reflections on Terrorism," *Foreign Affairs,* Fall 1986, p. 99.
2. Paul Wilkinson, *Terrorism and the Liberal State* (London: Macmillan Press, 1979), p. 93.
3. Ibid., p. 80.

PART I

The Terrorist Challenge to Democracies

THE LEVELS of press coverage of terrorism that may be acceptable in a democratic society are not only determined by the tactical exigencies of how best to resolve a specific incident with minimum loss of life, but are also governed by perceptions of the nature and level of the threat posed by terrorism to such a society. Differing interpretations of what terrorism is and how fundamentally it threatens society affect decisions on how governments may best react: differing perceptions give rise to differing views on the appropriate level and nature of government reaction, including associated changes that may be introduced in media practice, either through voluntary self-censorship or via government legislation.

Public awareness of the growing incidence of terrorist activity may be traced back to 1968, when the student rebellion in the United States and Europe along with events in the Middle East generated the first development of "modern terrorism." Statistics gathered by various agencies indicated an increase in the number of incidents throughout the 1970s and 1980s, paralleled by increases in the use of violence, in the numbers of casualties recorded annually, and of incidents in which multiple fatalities occurred. Although most terrorist events were concentrated in Western Europe, Latin America, and the Middle East, the nationality of victims showed a different pattern, the majority being citizens of North America and Western Europe. Attacks against diplomatic personnel, also principally from the Western liberal democracies, increased from fewer than a hundred in 1968 to more than four hundred per year in the early 1980s. The overall pattern was of terrorism targeted largely and specifically at Western democracies.

The evolution of terrorist activity constantly poses new problems for governments. The availability of sophisticated technology through normal retailing channels (e.g., timing devices) or in the international arms market (e.g., rocket launchers, ground-to-air missiles) has been exploited by terrorist groups. The possibility of terrorists gaining access to weapons of mass destruction, whether nuclear, chemical, or biological, gives cause for grave concern.

The dangerous potential of high technology is compounded by perceived changes in the nature and organization of terrorists. Within Western Europe the development of a "Euroterrorist network" has given particular cause for concern. Evidence exists of at least informal collaboration between the Red Army Faction, the Red Brigades, Action Direct, and the Belgian Fighting Communist Cells and their joint involvement in attacks against NATO personnel and installations. Perceptions of and reactions to this development were initially different in the countries affected, and countermeasures were limited in their effect and duration. But since then successes against the Red Brigades in Italy and terrorist cells in Belgium, France, and the Federal Republic of Germany have resulted in the capture of a significant number of activists. A resulting lull in European-generated terrorism has been noted, but involvement of Red Brigade members in terrorist activity in France indicates that too optimistic a view should not be taken. Although the existence of a coordinating committee for European terrorist activity has yet to be demonstrated, the informal contacts that undoubtedly have occurred provide a genuine potential for future problems in the region.

Problems posed by the evolution of coordinated terrorist activity have been compounded by the involvement of groups in drug-related operations, the association of extreme religious belief with some groups, and the sponsorship of others by nation-states. Narcoterrorism contributes to the criminalization of terrorism and provides substantial funding. Religious zeal may be seen as altering the parameters within which counterterrorist forces have to operate: suicide attacks associated with fanatical religious attitudes represent a new phenomenon. Such attacks have been linked, although not exclusively, with Islamic fundamentalism. State sponsorship of terrorism has provided training facilities, weaponry, tactical support, and safe havens for various groups. The degree to which states directly control groups involved is unclear, but their support has been crucial in a number of incidents.

The role of sponsorship from within the Communist bloc is also debated. The incidence of terrorism in Communist states is low, given the capacity for such societies to deal rigorously with potential terrorist groups. Few attacks against citizens of Communist states have been recorded. A pattern of decreasing terrorism has been noted during periods of East-West détente, as has increased activity when confrontation between the blocs increases. Linked with the provision of education and training facilities to terrorist groups, at least indirect sponsorship by Communist states has been mooted. The support of Communist states for national liberation movements, many of which are viewed as terroristic in the West, complicates the evaluation.

Western counterterrorist activity may be viewed as essentially practical, concerned less with the problem of understanding the terrorist than with eliminating the terrorist's impact on society. At this level, proposed actions include

- no negotiation under any circumstances;
- preemptive action against terrorists planning attacks;
- diplomatic, economic, and, in extreme cases, military pressure against state sponsors;
- the restructuring of diplomatic procedures to limit abuse in support of terrorism; and
- more and better international cooperation among governments, their relevant specialized agencies, and their intelligence networks.

Strong measures are justified on the ground that terrorism is a form of low-intensity warfare that should be treated accordingly without compromise. Understanding terrorism and its motivation is often considered useful only insofar as it enables society to react effectively against the threat.

The definition of terrorism as "war" raises issues that are linked closely with deciding how best to deal with it. In a war situation, negotiation and compromise are not acceptable. Other authorities view terrorism as a crime rather than an act of war, and the rules governing societies' reactions may therefore be different. At a practical level, for a government not to negotiate may be difficult, given the facts that it is unable to allow victims to be "sacrificed," that failure to respond may provoke increased and more extreme terrorist actions, and that such actions would adversely affect relations among states involved. Within this frame of reference, negotiation with terrorists may be seen as acceptable, provided the negotiators have established clear goals and have adequate information on the terrorists and their real aims.

Clearly, differences exist on how negotiations should proceed, on whether they should be tactical and designed to end a given situation, after which concessions may be withdrawn, or whether they should involve genuine dialogue. The proper nature of terrorist-negotiator relations is also debated, whether trust should be built up for use in possible future incidents or whether terrorists should be aware that they cannot trust the authorities to abide by agreements. The basic issue of how best to react—firmly and with force or through dialogue and accommodation—remains to be settled within the international community. Both approaches have been tried at various times by numerous governments; results have been mixed and neither method has been totally effective.

Conclusions on these issues influence perceptions of the "correct" role to be played by the media. The issue of press censorship regarding terrorism is central. Some argue that limited or no reporting is preferable, as it limits terrorist propaganda and enables counterterrorist agencies to operate effectively; others note that a lack of reporting serves only to undermine the credibility of the press and thus of democratic values in society. The capability of government to prevent reporting within a democratic state is also doubted. Censorship of the wartime variety is seen to be effective but may be considered too draconian in the face of terrorist activity. The commercial, competitive, and ideological nature of the press may also preclude effective self-censorship: one agency, newspaper, or TV station is always liable to break ranks and publish a story.

At the practical level, journalists note they are well aware of the issues but face difficult decisions. The interview of a terrorist leader may be considered of legitimate interest, providing the audience with information on which to evaluate the message of the group concerned. Others believe such interviews represent a propaganda success for the terrorists. A decision on whether to proceed involves a judgment as to whether the interview is harmful or informative; many argue that the role of the press is to report all points of view independently. Except when lives are at risk, government should not affect the decision if the press is to fulfill its central role in a democratic society of providing independent, truthful information to the population. However, the possibilities of collaborating to some degree with the authorities remain open, and the consequences for security cannot be ignored. Also, the fact that the terrorist is explicitly seeking to project a propaganda message through the media is to be recognized and due allowance made. The nature of propaganda efforts and the dilemmas they pose for the media are examined in chapter 1.

CHAPTER 1

Terrorism and International Security

The Right Honorable Lord Chalfont, OBE, MC

Since the lecture on which this text is based was delivered at Wilton Park at the beginning of 1988, important changes have occurred, both in the policies of the Soviet Union and in the activities of the PLO. Indeed, the picture of international terrorism has changed materially in the last year, and the following text should be read with that in mind.

LIBERAL DEMOCRACY of the kind to which we are accustomed is under a greater threat today than it has been at any time in this century—a threat greater even than that of the 1930s. The dangers come from different sources, all to some extent interconnected but worth examining as separate phenomena. The first is the growth of Soviet military power and the imperialist foreign policies that have accompanied it. The evidence of this development is now incontrovertible, yet still we have not fully comprehended its significance. A second source is internal disruption deriving from social unrest caused by a progressive lowering of national standards and morale and exploited ruthlessly by political extremists both of the Left and the Right. The third threat is possibly the most significant: international terrorism—a phenomenon that might pose a greater threat to democratic societies than either external military aggression or internal subversion. The great danger, of course, is that all three are capable of being used as instruments of destruction by political enemies.

An examination of international terrorism must include a review of the development of terrorism as an international phenomenon as opposed to something purely national or regional; it must consider the extent to which the media of communications, the press, and the mass media contribute in some ways to the success of the terrorist; and it should suggest some measures the international community can take to deal with what is now a major worldwide problem.

First of all, in the interests of clarity and understanding, we must attempt to define the topic. What precisely is terrorism? Can we demonstrate that it has become an international phenomenon? Some suggest that no definition of terrorism is needed, that terrorism is like some monstrously ugly and frightening wild animal we might not be able to describe or define, but would recognize immediately if it appeared. Lenin, who might be regarded as something of an expert on the subject, once said quite simply that "the aim of terrorism is to terrify." Nevertheless, in the interest of intellectual clarity, a definition is required:

> Terrorism is the deliberate, systematic murder, maiming, or menacing of the innocent to inspire fear in order to gain political ends.

This definition is fairly comprehensive and accurate but not exhaustive. We would need to say many other things about terrorism before we could study it intelligently and in depth. Paul Johnson's pamphlet *The Seven Deadly Sins of Terrorism* discusses some of them. However, having arrived at a serviceable definition, a number of things must be said about this phenomenon before we can fully appreciate the effects it has on people's lives. Terrorism, as Johnson has written, has a number of significant characteristics. The first is that it idealizes violence. For the soldier or the police officer, violence is a necessary evil. For the terrorist, violence is something admirable in itself, a desirable form of activity. This fact derives from the teachings of certain modern philosophers such as Jean-Paul Sartre and Frantz Fanon, who have preached a gospel of violence summed up in the words of Fanon, who said, "Violence is a cleansing force: it frees the oppressed from their despair." This nihilistic philosophy emphasizes the fact that for most terrorists violence is not a last resort but a desirable and idealized form of action.

A second point is that terrorism rejects the kind of morality familiar to everyone. No one can be a successful terrorist so long as he or she adheres to the moral principles of an ordinary, civilized human being.

The third characteristic is that terrorism rejects the political process. This feature is perhaps not sufficiently understood. People talk about terrorism as political violence; indeed, it is often carried out in the pursuit of some political aim. We therefore tend to think of terrorism as part of a political process, but it is not. It is a *substitute* for the political process. Terrorism is totally divorced from and hostile to the whole concept of the political process. Instead, it subscribes to the totalitarian belief that the most effective way of destroying an idea is to destroy the person who holds it. This process is not political in any acceptable sense of the word.

The next important point is that terrorism promotes totalitarianism. A tendency among certain modern political philosophers is to think that terrorism is in some way neutral between democracy on one hand and anarchy or totalitarianism on the other. It is not. Terrorism does not tend toward anarchy or toward democracy; it tends toward totalitarianism. It actively and systematically assists the spread of the totalitarian idea.

It follows that terrorism threatens only democratic systems. There is no terrorism in Bulgaria. There is no terrorism in Cuba. There is no terrorism in the Soviet Union. There is no terrorism of any effective kind in any totalitarian state. Terrorism can destroy, and has destroyed, democracies. It cannot destroy, and probably will never destroy, a totalitarian state.

Perhaps most important of all, terrorism undermines the will of civilized society to defend itself. People all have an instinctive desire to defend their freedom, their way of life, and the values of their civilization. Terrorism deliberately undermines it. Carlos Mirejeva, the Brazilian terrorism theorist, said that terrorism has two aims in a political system: first, to make life unbearable for ordinary people; and second, to create a climate of collapse. Terrorists set out to undermine the general will of civilized society to defend itself and to make people so sick and tired of violence and indiscriminate bloodshed that they lose their will to defend themselves.

If one accepts the definition of terrorism as formulated above and adds to it the factors outlined, terrorism is not a marginal problem. It is not something that lives in the periphery of people's lives, nor is it something that is part of the ordinary processes of society. Terrorism cannot be regarded as one of the manifestations of modern society to be placed alongside things like football hooliganism, the indiscipline of the young, and the various aberrations of modern industrial society. When a terrorist commits an act of atrocity in our society, sometimes we hear, "We are all guilty." We are *not* all guilty. Terrorism is a specific problem that can be identified and is not just a frustrating problem with which people have to learn to live. We must learn *not* to live with it. Terrorism is a real and a growing danger to the very survival of legitimate states—any state that lives under the rule of law.

During the period when international terrorism has existed as a phenomenon, say, the last twenty-five years, it has been largely a left-wing, that is, Marxist or Communist-oriented, movement. However, a new development is the growth of terrorism on the extreme Right. It is not yet the major threat that left-wing terrorism is, but it is enough to look at some events of the 1980s: The attack on a synagogue in Paris, the terrible incident at the Bologna railway station, and the appalling outrage at the Oktoberfest in Munich. These acts were, as far as anyone can confirm at the moment, committed by openly declared right-wing terrorist organizations. They should be a warning that international terrorism is not quite as simple and not quite as easy to identify as we might have thought.

Axel Springer, writing in *Die Zeit,* put it in a very stark and perturbing way: "We are now facing an unholy alliance between anti-Semitism and anti-Zionism." Now, whether that statement is true or not, note that a leader of a German right-wing terrorist organization has been trained in the Fatah camp in Lebanon. This development is profoundly disturbing. We cannot afford to ignore it; it is the way that new directions begin. At the moment it is just a dark cloud on the horizon.

With its special nature, however, and its special targets, right-wing terrorism is only a facet of the wider problem of international terrorism. The overall question we must consider is, How can a civilized world deal with this problem?

The first thing to be understood is that terrorism is now an international phenomenon in every sense of the word. Three tests can be applied to demonstrate that it has now become international in scope. The first is that areas of activity are no longer confined within national frontiers. Terrorists no longer observe national frontiers, except the frontiers of totalitarian police states—where they know they would not last very long. The second test is the systematic and worldwide network of collaboration among terrorist organizations, whatever their own aims may be. Whether their aims are religious, ethnic, or nationalist, they have links all over the world. The third and perhaps most important point is that the international terror is aided, protected, and financed by a number of governments in pursuit of their own political ends.

Let us look at each of the tests in a little more detail. We have hardly any need to spend time demonstrating that the sphere of terrorist activity is now international and has no regard for national frontiers. We have only to look at the activities of the PLO, Libyan terrorists, or Iraqi terrorists in London; the attack by Japanese on passengers at Lod Airport; the attack on the synagogue in Paris; the activities in the Netherlands of the South Moluccans, who must have known that the government of the Netherlands could have no effect upon their political grievance at all and yet visited this terror upon the Dutch people, not upon their own government; the Irish Republican Army (IRA) operating in Western Europe; and, of course, the attempt on the life of the pope by a Turkish gunman.

Another indication is the indiscriminate hijacking of aircraft of any airline anywhere in the world if it will serve the ends of the terrorists. We have reached the stage where countries and cities with no connection of any kind to the aims of the terrorists have become battlegrounds. Now innocent citizens—not only of the governments with whom terrorists have some kind of quarrel but also of any country in the world—are at risk from alien and menacing murderers.

The international links among the terrorist groups are perhaps not generally known or easily recognized. They are nevertheless well established and documented. These links have nothing to do with any community of political, religious, or nationalist ideology. The IRA may have nothing politically in common with the Baader-Meinhof gang or with the Palestine Liberation Organization (PLO). Nevertheless, they share everything that makes their operations successful; they exchange weapons, engage in joint operational planning, use each other's training areas, and provide each other with administrative and logistic support.

The principal groups involved in this are familiar: the Japanese Red Army; the Baader-Meinhof gang, as it was once called until it was succeeded by the Red Army Faction; the Iranian Fedayeen; the IRA; a number of Latin American groups, such as the Tupamaros of Uruguay and the Montoneros of Argentina; and, of course, the extreme right-wing groups already mentioned.

Behind them all has been the central organization in the whole network of international terrorism: the PLO and the Popular Front for the Liberation of Palestine (PFLP). That the PFLP has received assistance of every kind from clandestine organizations in at least fourteen countries is clearly and incontrovertibly documented. In exchange, they have given aid to a number of other terrorist organizations. The Baader-Meinhof gang was trained at the Fatah camps in Lebanon and Syria in 1970. The Red Army Faction was trained in South Yemen and has taken part in a number of PFLP operations, including the Entebbe hijacking in 1976 and the attacks on the Organization of Petroleum Exporting Countries (OPEC) ministers in Vienna in 1979. The Italian Red Brigades have collaborated with the Red Army Faction in Germany, for example, in a joint operation to kidnap an Austrian industrialist, almost certainly with Arab support. Interrogation of the people who murdered Aldo Moro in Italy provided information that a member of the gang that murdered him was trained and instructed by the PLO. The February 1978 murder of an Egyptian journalist in Cyprus clearly linked a Palestinian group based in Iraq and the Red Brigades of Italy. Of the seven people arrested as a result of the murder of that Egyptian journalist, one was German, one was Swiss, three were Palestinians, and two were Jordanians.

In the days leading up to the revolution in Iran, the Iranian Fedayeen, who collaborated with the Islamic revolutionaries in bringing down the shah, received financial support, propaganda material, and training from Colonel Muammar Khaddafi in Libya. They had a station that broadcast propaganda twenty-four hours a day from the Soviet Union just over the Iranian border.

In addition, many examples of training cooperation can be cited. The Japanese at Lod Airport were trained in Syria and Lebanon. Weapons and equipment have been exchanged. The systematic organization of international terrorism is clear beyond any doubt. Once the fashionable response was, "Oh, of course, they help each other from time to time. After all, they have similar aims. Why shouldn't they? But there's nothing sinister about it." Nevertheless, something *is* sinister about this carefully coordinated international activity that operates irrespective of the alleged aims of the specific terrorist organizations. As a result of this international collaboration, the incidence of terrorism has grown alarmingly in recent years. No other tenable explanation can account for the increase. In the whole of 1965, fewer than twenty terrorist incidents were recorded. In 1978 the count was more than three hundred, and in 1988 more than a thousand. The incidence of terrorism has therefore increased in a dramatic way in the last ten to fifteen years.

We must be concerned not only with the fact that terrorism has international links but also with its state paymasters. Terrorists could not conduct their operations unless someone behind them provided the planning, the direction, the intelligence, the weapons, and the money. As noted earlier, terrorism tends toward the establishment and perpetuation of totalitarianism. Therefore, we should not be surprised that the countries that finance and maintain the international terrorist networks are totalitarian states; they use these organizations to pursue their own political aims. Libya supports, finances, and helps terrorist organizations throughout the world. Arms and training, safe havens, false passports, and funds come not only from Libya but also from South Yemen, Algeria, Iraq, Syria, and many other countries in the Middle East.

The real sponsors of international terrorism, however, are the Soviet Union and the Eastern European countries of the Soviet bloc. We should begin from the premise that these countries have no separate foreign policies. The Soviet Union controls all intelligence and international actions in the Soviet bloc. The head of the Cuban Secret Service is a Russian officer. All East European secret intelligence agencies report directly to the State Security Committee (KGB) in Moscow. Anything they do is approved by and controlled from the KGB in Moscow. The Soviet Union itself, beginning with its activities in the Lenin Institute and the Patrice Lumumba University down through its surrogates in Cuba, North Korea, South Yemen, Angola, and the East European satellites, controls and directs the supply of arms, training, and KGB intelligence for the terrorist organizations of the world. In the Soviet Union, a fully developed terrorist infrastructure is integrated into the foreign-policy machine. The International Department of the Central Committee of the Communist Party of the Soviet Union is responsible for the Lenin Institute and Patrice Lumumba University; the KGB engages in clandestine penetration of other terrorist organizations around the world, as does the Soviet military intelligence organization (GRU). Terrorist organizations from all over the world have training camps in at least three Soviet cities: Baku, Tashkent, and Odessa. Some of the subjects of training at the Patrice Lumumba University are agitation and propaganda, sabotage, street fighting, and the techniques of assassination—presumably, all part of the liberal arts syllabus.

Examples of direct Soviet involvement in the activities of national terrorist movements have been clearly documented. The Baader-Meinhof Group in Germany that most people thought was anti-Marxist and that was indeed openly critical of and hostile to the Soviet Union was in fact subsidized in its activities by the government of East Germany, which in turn got its directions from the KGB. The Red Army Faction, which succeeded the Baader-Meinhof gang, was founded by the man who edited *Konkret,* a magazine of the extreme Left. He was also married to Ulrike Meinhof of the Baader-Meinhof gang, and that organization was heavily subsidized by East Germany and Czechoslovakia. In 1971 a large consignment of Russian arms consigned to the IRA was seized at Schiphol Airport in the Netherlands. In 1973 the SS *Claudia* was seized by the Irish police with five tons of Soviet arms, ammunition, and equipment on board.

Terrorists are no longer—if they ever were—a fragmented, amateur, inefficient collection of mindless thugs around the world. The picture that emerges today is of a ruthless and pitiless movement of violent men and women. Some of them are undoubtedly psychopathic, but many of them are not. They have a comprehensive network of international contacts. They are sponsored, armed, financed, and in many cases directed by the Soviet

Union. One of the added dangers of all this—because terrorists are financed and equipped from the outside—is that they now have at their disposal sophisticated and advanced weapons. That various small terrorist groups now have access to Soviet missiles capable of shooting down not only military aircraft but civil airliners as well is a new and disturbing phenomenon.

Up to now the cozy fallacy in the West has been that terrorism is some kind of spontaneous outburst of emotive and mindless protest and that while it may be unpleasant and violent it is at least directed against the repressive forces in society. The truth, in fact, is precisely the reverse. International terrorism depends for its existence on just those repressive forces; it depends upon police states, and it is directed at the political institutions and social systems of democratic states.

The part played in this problem by the press, broadcasting, and television requires examination. Before we can fight terrorism effectively, we have to establish a sympathetic and supportive climate of public opinion. One of the principal instruments in achieving this ought to be the free press and communications media of the West. The depressing fact, however, is that newspapers, radio, and television have probably done more than the terrorist organizations themselves to make organized political violence glamorous and successful.

The first point to be grasped is that terrorism would be impotent without publicity. It depends for its effect upon dramatic impact in order to compel and hold public attention. Terrorists have occasionally shown great sophistication in manipulating the media. Some of the results have been striking and disturbing. The National Liberation Front (FLN) in Algeria discovered that if ten Frenchmen were killed in the desert no one noticed, but one killed in the Casbah would be front-page news the next day in every Paris newspaper. Perhaps the most illuminating case history in this context is the Symbionese Liberation Army (SLA), which sprang into prominence in California as a result of the Patty Hearst case. For months the SLA received massive exposure on television and the press, their tape recordings were broadcast over the radio networks in circumstances of maximum drama, and a massive operation involving a great number of police and Federal Bureau of Investigation (FBI) agents was mounted to search for them. Yet this terrifying organization never consisted of more than a dozen people, and its exploits—apart from the sensational abduction of Miss Hearst—were no more than small-time criminal operations. It was amplified into an important political phenomenon almost entirely by the attention of the media.

We must admit, of course, that violence makes good copy. A machine-gun attack on a bank makes exciting reading, and in a free press journalists report and editors print what they believe to be exciting for their readers. Yet the matter cannot be allowed to rest there because in this particular context the freedom of the press is being consistently abused or at least manipulated cynically and irresponsibly.

Of course, some journalists actively sympathize with the criminal activities of terrorist movements, especially those dedicated to the destruction of

capitalist societies. Others assist less consciously in the promotion of terrorism by accepting terrorist organizations at their own value and adopting the
kind of newspeak George Orwell made so familiar in his *1984*. Terrorists are
referred to as "commandos," "urban guerrillas," or even "freedom fighters"; an organization dedicated to the violent overthrow of an elected government becomes the "Patriotic Front"; IRA murders in Northern Ireland
are reported as "executions"; and the brutal tortures of soldiers and civilians are termed "trials" or "interrogations".

At the same time, the tendency is to search for some kind of bogus intellectual objectivity and to regard the terrorist on the one hand, and the police
officer or soldier on the other, as two sides of a morally symmetrical confrontation. In publications of otherwise impeccable respectability, the
phrase "state violence" is used to describe military or police action against
violent subversives and terrorists. This language often results from the sheer
incapacity to distinguish between an attack by a violent minority on the institutions of a democratic state and the right of that state to defend itself against
such an attack. This absence of differentiation is demonstrated by the frequent television appearances of terrorists and the spokespeople of the organizations that sponsor them, who are allowed to disseminate their violent
propaganda with the same freedom as a candidate for Parliament addressing
his or her constituency.

As a result, many reasonable people—especially among the young—
have failed to understand the true nature of the terrorist threat that imperils
their survival. This failure of understanding creates a climate of opinion in
which political leaders and the commanders of security forces cannot act
decisively in a terrorist situation; in this special context, the balance between freedom and order must be subjected to constant reappraisal. The
press and other communications media of the free world should, as a matter
of great urgency, reexamine their attitudes to subversion and international
terrorism. They should realize that their freedom is conditional upon the
larger freedom of the society in which they exist; when the larger freedom
is destroyed, their own will disappear with it. This caution is not meant to
suggest that news of terrorist activities should not be reported but that the
incidents should be reported coldly, factually, and deprived of their excitement and glamor. Gunmen and bombers should not be interviewed respect-
fully as though they were delivering an address on the state of the nation,
and those who seek a totally fallacious moral symmetry in their editorializing
should remember that their precious freedom to report and to comment is
always one of the first casualties of the descent into totalitarianism.

The only alternative to some kind of self-regulation in these matters is
interference by the state. At this very suggestion, great cries of outrage will
be heard emerging from the newspaper offices and television studios. Yet
in wartime the free nations of the world willingly accept a degree of press
censorship designed to prevent damage to national security. Unless newspaper editors and those who control radio and television programs are prepared to give evidence of a greater sense of responsibility than they have

shown in the past, the pressure for some kind of legislative regulation over the reporting of terrorism and the interviewing of terrorists is bound to increase.

The special position of the British Broadcasting Corporation (BBC) and the way it discharges its responsibilities require examination. The BBC is not in the same position as a newspaper or even as commercial television. The BBC holds a unique position, one in which holding a corporate political view is not permissible, yet such a view exists. Over the whole spectrum of domestic programs, on both radio and television, the general bias is against the status quo and the established order; at best the attitude is magisterial, as though the Corporation occupies some lofty and evenhanded position between the established order on the one hand and the terrorist, the hooligan, and the extremist on the other. Some IRA terrorists are interviewed; producers negotiate with illegal organizations in the interests of putting on a program; no attempt is made to ensure that the presence of microphones and cameras does not, in itself, provoke violence. Totally disproportionate publicity has been given to hunger strikers and to the theatrical semimilitary burial services that follow their deaths. The predictable justification is the great god News and the pervasive fallacy of "the public's right to know."

When the director-general of the BBC was challenged on this point, he referred to the remarkable publicity given to the convicted terrorist known with cozy familiarity as "Bobby Sands"; the director-general said that the event of "an elected member of Parliament starving himself to death was uniquely newsworthy." This response seems to betray the existence of a bizarre set of values in the higher direction of the BBC. Sir Ian Trethowan went on to say, in response to a question about the provocative nature of such television coverage, "There was violence before television." This attitude misses the point and typifies a reluctance on the part of the BBC to admit that it might be failing entirely to live up to its responsibilities, its traditions, and its role in a free and orderly society.

In dealing with terrorism, the question of media involvement has to come very high on the list. Almost all solutions ultimately depend on the way they are communicated to people throughout the world who rely upon the information system provided by the mass media. Solving the problem of terrorism depends on several requirements. The first is to recognize the threat as international. Second, the corruption of language must be resisted. Freedom fighters don't blow up school buses; murderers do. Freedom fighters don't murder innocent businessmen going about their lawful trade; murderers do that. Liberation movements don't set fire to farmhouses; terrorists do. Terrorists don't interrogate prisoners; they torture them. Terrorists don't execute informers; they murder their fellows. When the body of an IRA terrorist who has committed suicide in prison is taken to the front room of his parents' house to await burial, he is not, as the BBC described it, "lying in state." When a handful of masked thugs discharge their Russian rifles over his grave, it is not "a funeral with full military honors." Language must be used precisely because language, after all, is not just a crude method of communication within a species. Language is something more definitive and much more precise.

The next requirement is to expose constantly the sponsors of international terrorism. When the PLO, the IRA, the Red Army, or the Red Brigades throw a bomb, let us ask, Who provided the bomb and who trained the terrorists? Where did they go to school? Where did they get their equipment? The sponsors of terrorism must be exposed before world opinion. The conspiracy of silence that seems to have existed in the past must be ended.

Next, the protectors of terrorism must be punished. We must have really effective sanctions against nations that provide havens for hijackers and terrorists. The Hague Convention, the Tokyo Convention, and the Montreal Convention are supposed to deal with this problem. None of them do. Effective international legislation to deal with things like air piracy are needed. Intelligence systems, police systems, and planning must be centralized. Above all, one must *never* negotiate with terrorists.

International terrorism has assumed frightening dimensions in the last fifteen years. Paul Johnson, at a conference on international terrorism in Jerusalem in 1979, said,

> Terrorism is the greatest evil of our age, a more serious threat to our culture and survival than the possibility of nuclear war, or even the rapid depletion of the planet's resources. Civilization not only has the right, but a positive and imperative duty to defend itself. We are the beneficiaries of the past and, more importantly, the trustees of the future.

I believe that to be true. The quality and texture of our lives have been transformed and degraded by this squalid phenomenon of international terrorism. We must take action against it.

> Free men, if they are willing to fight, if they are ready to employ their courage and wisdom, and channel all their resources into a concerted action, can always overcome ruthless evil, however dreadful or threatening.

That quotation is from Benjamin Netanyahu, Israel's deputy foreign minister and the brother of Jonathan Netanyahu, who was killed at Entebbe.

The media, especially the BBC, must be persuaded to recognize that they have a clear and unequivocal responsibility on one side of this confrontation. They should concentrate a little less on the faults of the established order and a little more on the forces that threaten to destroy our society.

One of the more distinguished American journalists has already accepted this. In a column in the *Washington Post,* George Will wrote a short time ago:

> We of the Western press have yet to come to terms with international terrorism. If we thought about it more and understood its essence we would probably stop writing about it or we would write about it with a great deal more respect. And many of the terrorists and would-be terrorists would fade away.

Another way of saying that was put to me some years ago by Sir William Haley, editor of *The Times* when I joined it in 1961. Shortly after I joined, we were having an editorial conference and were discussing a problem very much of this kind. After Sir William had given his views about how we in *The Times* were going to deal with it, someone else in the meeting said, "But surely, Sir William, you must realize that there are two sides to every conflict." Haley fixed him with a very cold eye, and said, "No, young man, there are not two sides to every question. Some things are evil and cruel and ugly and no amount of fine writing on your part will make them good or kind or beautiful."

Sir William Haley was not only editor of *The Times* but also director-general of the BBC. I warmly commend his words, as well as his values and his principles, to his successors in both institutions.

PART II

Terrorism as Propaganda

T HE USE of violence for propaganda is crucial to terrorist activity. The critical role of propaganda is recognized by terrorists who commit considerable planning and organizational resources to it. Political wings have been established by many
terrorist groups to bolster their propaganda activity. Whereas governments seek to control terrorism through police and intelligence activity, they are required also to conduct a counterpropaganda campaign
to maintain or extend support for the regime and diminish that for the
terrorists. However, the very nature of terrorist violence often seems
counterproductive in that it tends to strengthen resistance, provoke
public outrage and dislike, generate strong counterterrorist measures,
and brand perpetrators as inhumane, which undermines their claim
to legitimacy.

Partially as a result of this contradiction between the terrorist's
desire for legitimacy and the adverse reaction of the public (also for
psychological reasons, as explained below), terrorists adopt attitudes
that enable them to reconcile the resulting dilemmas. These include
(1) a belief that their cause is righteous and therefore their methods
are justified; (2) an unqualified hatred for the enemy that opposes
them; (3) a belief that the justice of their cause is such that its eventual
triumph is inevitable even if not achievable in the short term; and (4)
a moral certainty in the cause that enables them to deny that their
acts are criminal and to justify their belief that terror is a legitimate
method of coercion. As a result of this mind-set, they are able to

justify their actions to themselves. Violence becomes a praiseworthy activity in itself and a justified reaction to the repression of the authorities. Their perception is that their war will be protracted, that survival will of itself lead to victory, and that the government may succeed only if it does so quickly and totally. Attitudes toward the authorities stress the need to arouse a sense of guilt within the establishment and to stress the authorities' untrustworthiness and the incompetence of their security forces, which are to be terrorized to undermine their morale. Core aims are to undermine the legitimacy of the regime and to establish the credibility of the terrorist strategy.

To undermine the government, terrorists seek to demonstrate that the activities of security forces are counterproductive and ineffective. They will seek a special status, whatever crimes are committed; this status is to be accorded without the terrorists observing basic standards of acceptable behavior. They seek to demonstrate that security and protection may be offered by their group rather than the government. This series of attitudes and related objectives provide core elements in terrorist propaganda. To counter it effectively, the media has to offer alternative views and information. A government faced with the primary responsibility for organizing resistance to terrorism is faced with the question of how best to conduct counterpropaganda using the avenues available in liberal democracies through an independent media.

To achieve this, clear goals and acceptable methods have to be defined. In the liberal democratic state, both the government and its citizens must necessarily have the political will to resist; government action should be consistent with this goal. Although resources and professionalism are required to combat terrorism on the ground, resources are also required to win the propaganda contest and thus to maintain popular support. Events must be correctly reported and the public must be informed, subject to security-related restrictions that are frequently a matter of contention between media and government. The lies and atrocities of the terrorists have to be revealed and publicized to take advantage of the fact that support for terrorist goals within society is generally limited and support for their methods even more restricted. Overreaction to terrorism through crude censorship may only undermine the credibility of the government and security forces. Public support is crucial, and a constructive relationship with the media is therefore essential to conduct the required dissemination of information.

Many argue that the media similarly have responsibilities to society; they must seek to avoid manipulation by the terrorists to their propaganda advantage. Self-control in reporting events is therefore required. However, the practical application of such general propositions inevitably generates differences between governments, primarily concerned with curbing terrorism, and the media, whose prime responsibility is to report news and information.

CHAPTER 2

Terrorism and Propaganda

Paul Wilkinson

DEFINITION AND CHARACTERISTICS OF TERRORIST VIOLENCE

The history of terrorism totally disproves Hannah Arendt's claim that violence is speechless.[1] Terrorist propaganda is sometimes crude and callow, but it can also be extremely skillful and effective. All serious terrorist campaigns are characterized by frenetic use of every available access to the mass media. Some groups have set up their own radio stations; others have produced videos of their captive hostages to increase the pressure on the governments they seek to blackmail. In democratic states, a typical terrorist organ for waging this form of political warfare is a political party wing that can, if necessary, continue to operate legally if and when the terrorist organization itself is proscribed. Obviously, the terrorists' scope for this type of political propaganda activity is severely limited under an authoritarian political system, although it is worth recalling that Ayatollah Khomeini managed to sustain an extremely effective covert propaganda campaign against the shah's rule, even from exile in Iraq and Paris, including the use of tape-recorded propaganda sermons smuggled into Iran for use by the mullahs. In liberal democratic societies, the major terrorist organizations can make maximum use of the freedoms of speech and press that prevail. In a healthy and vigorous liberal democracy, they are unlikely to win majority approval for the use of terrorism, but they may hope to win substantial backing for some of their broader political aims and to weaken or neutralize support for those who oppose them. At the very least, the terrorist organization is aware that its own recruitment, support base, and influence, at home and abroad, are crucially affected by this political battle for legitimacy and moral support.

Here the major forms of justification put forward by terrorists and their supporters are identified and examined and their implications discussed. Many of these attempts have a superficial plausibility. Underestimating the degree to which they may succeed in deluding sections of public opinion would be foolish. Even though terrorist propagandists have not succeeded in getting their myths and doctrines generally accepted, they have often suc-

26

ceeded in confusing politicians and the public and thereby in undermining the political will and unity needed to oppose terrorism effectively.

One major source of confusion has been the definition of terrorism. A common statement is that any generally agreed-upon definition of terrorism is impossible and that because one cannot be sure of what it means, discussing policies to deal with it is useless. Many political and strategic concepts are difficult to define in a few sentences. Concepts such as democracy, imperialism, and revolution, for example, have been used in many different ways, but does this mean we can simply dispense with them? Of course not, because a sufficient common understanding of the meanings of these terms makes them useful, indeed essential, in scholarly discourse and political debate.

In any case, the problems of establishing a degree of common understanding of the concept of terrorism have been vastly exaggerated. Indeed, I suspect that some have tried to deny that any common usage exists as a device for obstructing cooperation in policies to combat terrorism. Those who still genuinely believe that definition is a fundamental obstacle to the investigation of terrorist phenomena have clearly failed to study the growing academic literature, the proceedings of international scholarly conferences, and the modest but significant advances in international law and cooperation in this field. In a recent paper Jeffrey Ross and Ted Gurr draw attention to Alex Schmid's thorough international review[2] of the definitional problem.

> After an exhaustive analysis of over 100 expert definitions Schmid concludes that there is no "true or correct definition." Nevertheless, he develops a consensus definition consisting of five parts which we accept for our purposes. First, terrorism is a method of combat in which random or symbolic victims are targets of violence. Second, through previous use of violence or the credible threat of violence, other members of that group or class are put in a state of chronic fear. Third, the victimization of the target is considered extranormal by most observers, which fourth, creates an audience beyond the target of terror. Fifth, the purpose of terrorism is either to immobilize the target of terror in order to produce disorientation and/or compliance, or to mobilize secondary targets of demands (e.g., government) or targets of attention (e.g., public opinion). This definition encompasses terrorism by governments, by oppositions, and by international movements.[3]

Terrorism can be briefly defined as coercive intimidation or more fully as the systematic use of murder, injury, and destruction or threat of same to create a climate of terror, to publicize a cause, and to coerce a wider target into submitting to its aims. International terrorism is terrorism exported across international frontiers or used against foreign targets in the terrorists' country of origin. Purely domestic terrorism is relatively rare, but in many campaigns the political violence is mainly concentrated in a single territory or region (for example, in the cases of the IRA and the Basque and Corsican terrorists).

A major characteristic of political terror is its indiscriminate nature, which is not to deny that terrorists generally have a specific human target, whether individual or collective, that is intended to be the victim of the most direct physical harm. Quite apart from the danger of those who are not pre-selected targets being hurt is the unavoidable side effect of widespread fear that others might be harmed. As Raymond Aron remarks in one of his most percipient observations on terror:

> An action of violence is labelled "terrorist" when its psychological effects are out of proportion to its purely physical result. In this sense, the so-called indiscriminate acts of revolutionaries are terrorist, as were the Anglo-American zone bombings. The lack of discrimination helps to spread fear, for if no one in particular is a target, no one can be safe.[4]

Terrorists are frequently prepared to engage in the indiscriminate murder of civilians. Men, women, and children alike, regardless of their role or position in society, may be regarded as potential victims for the sake of the cause. As a policy, the waging of terror necessarily involves disregarding the rules and conventions of war; noncombatants, hostages, prisoners of war, and neutrals have no inviolable rights in their eyes.

Acts of terror also characteristically appear entirely unpredictable and arbitrary to the society that suffers them. One writer has expressed this point very clearly "No observance of commands, no matter how punctilious, on the part of the prospective victims can ensure their safety."[5] Of course, in many instances individual victims of terroristic assassination or mass murder are given preliminary warning that they are to die. The point is that such warnings are only selective and predictable according to the rationalizations of the terrorists. As André Malraux writes, *"Le terroriste décidât seul exécutât seul,"*[6] (The terrorist decides on his own, executes on his own) and in this sense terrorism is a peculiar kind of tyranny in which the potential victim is unable to do anything to avoid destruction because the terrorist is operating and judging on the basis of an idiosyncratic code of rules and values. These characteristics of unpredictability and arbitrariness also apply in the case of the repressive terror of the state for two major reasons. First, leaders and agencies of force in the state, who have acquired the preponderance of coercive power, may disregard the underlying values and norms of the existing law with impunity within their domain. Second, tyrannical dictators of totalitarian governments tend, in the process of consolidating their power, to subvert and manipulate the legal structure in order to forge it into a weapon for the oppression of their internal opponents. Such regimes instinctively use terror as an instrument of domestic and foreign policy. Their terror is far more lethal and large-scale than that of substate actors, and for international opinion to alleviate or prevent large-scale violation of human rights by states is notoriously difficult.

What fundamentally distinguishes terrorism from other forms of organized violence is not simply its severity but also its features of amorality and antinomianism. Terrorists either profess indifference to existing moral codes or else claim exemption from all such obligations. Political terror, if it is waged consciously and deliberately, is implicitly prepared to sacrifice all moral and humanitarian consideration for the sake of some political end. Ideologies of terrorism assume that the death and suffering of those who are innocent of any crime are means entirely justified by their political ends. In their most explicit and candidly amoral form, such terrorist rationalizations amount to a Nietzschean doctrine of the will to power. Might is right, terror can always be justified as the expediency of the strong, and such Judeo-Christian notions as mercy, compassion, and conscience must go with the weak to the wall of history. Political terror is not always justified in such explicit terms. Some utopian or messianic sects and movements that have resorted to terror have attempted a teleological justification, generally involving the rejection of all existing ethical principles and codes on the grounds that morality is manipulated in the interests of the rulers. In some cases acts of terror are argued to be necessary sacrifices to be made on the journey toward a new revolutionary order that will introduce a new man, a new order, and a revolutionary morality, but the first task is to destroy the existing order and morality; terrorist propaganda is a key weapon in that task.

TERRORIST PROPAGANDA OF JUSTIFICATION

Very few systematic studies have been made of the propaganda and self-justifications used by the major terrorist organizations themselves. In an invaluable pioneering comparative study, Maurice Tugwell[7] has developed a powerful model that can be applied equally well to the terrorist propaganda of factions and of terror regimes. Certain elements in his model provide a valuable insight into the ways terrorist ideology is used to provide a new, transcendental "revolutionary justification," cleverly designed to subvert and destroy the moral and legal values that underpin the existing order.

In this propaganda war, the terrorists constantly emphasize the absolute justice or righteousness of their cause. Usually, this claim of justice is founded on a secular ideology. However, today we should note the significance of the resurgence of religious justifications for terrorism. Beliefs like those of the pro-Iranian fundamentalist terrorists—that acts of violence are ordained by God and that martyrdom in the course of the struggle against the infidel leads to Paradise—present a very potent threat to opponents. Whether based on secular ideology or religious faith, however, this belief in the absolute justice of the cause characterizes the propaganda of all terrorist organizations.

These beliefs carry some important corollaries. First, the terrorists can and do claim that because their violence is in a just cause they are freedom fighters or soldiers of liberation fighting a just war, and they passionately deny that their acts can be described as crimes or murders. Second, because of their belief in their own righteousness, the terrorists can portray their opponents not as simply misguided but as totally evil, as corrupt oppressors beyond redemption. Because their enemies are corrupt beyond redemption, the terrorists have the duty to kill them and indeed anyone who resists or obstructs the just war of the terrorists.

Third, because the terrorist organization believes it is waging a Manichean struggle with the forces of oppression or reaction, it cannot tolerate neutrals: "You must be either with us or against us. If you are with us, join our cause and fight against the enemy. If you are not actively with us, we will assume you are a traitor, and therefore we are entitled to kill you."

Three other key propaganda themes that can be derived from the Tugwell model vividly illustrate the potency of the terrorists' use of the claim of total righteousness as a psychological weapon. For example, it is used to undermine all claims to legitimacy on the part of the incumbents: "Our enemies, by denying the justice of our cause and by acting against us, have forfeited all rights to obedience and respect. It is no longer they who are legitimate and whose authority and word you should believe, but we the terrorist organization." The righteousness theme is also deployed in order to push the blame for all the violence onto the terrorists' opponents. The terrorist organization always claims that not they but the state, or their rival movement, started the violence: "Our violence was simply a totally justified reaction to the violence imposed on us by our enemies; hence, all the blame for the sufferings caused to the people should be placed on our opponents. The masses should recognize this and throw in their lot with our movement, which will inevitably triumph in the end." All these themes can be recognized in the propaganda of numerous contemporary terrorist organizations. We should never underestimate their skill in disseminating these illusions among the public and among politicians and other influential groups. At its most subtle and effective, this form of propaganda campaign may more than compensate for the military weaknesses and security failures of a terrorist organization. If governments, faced with these more sophisticated challenges, do not succeed in dealing effectively with the terrorists' political and psychological subversion, they may indeed be on the slide to disaster.

REDUCING THE TERRORISTS' OXYGEN

The recent history of terrorism in many democratic countries vividly demonstrates that terrorists thrive on the oxygen of publicity. Terrorists have used TV, radio, and the tabloid press for four main objectives:

1. To convey the propaganda of the deed and to create extreme fear among their target group

2. To mobilize wider support for their cause among the general population and international opinion by emphasizing such themes as the righteousness of their cause and the inevitability of their victory

3. To frustrate and disrupt the response of the government and security forces, for example, by suggesting that all their practical antiterrorist

measures are inherently tyrannical and counterproductive or an unnecessary overreaction

4. To mobilize, incite, and boost their constituency of actual and potential supporters and in so doing to increase recruitment, raise more funds, and inspire further attacks

Modern media technology has made the terrorists' task all too easy. In a few minutes, a terrorist group can place its signature on an atrocity and have its claims beamed around the world. The Munich Olympics massacre of 1972 was beamed to an estimated worldwide audience of more than 500 million. What can be done in free societies to limit this enormous media power of the terrorist is hard to know, except to establish greater self-restraint among the media managers and journalists.

The terrorists, working through their political wings and their own often highly experienced propagandists, can also relatively easily get some of their general propaganda into the mass media. Such propagandizing does not necessarily involve infiltrating fully trained terrorist activists into media organizations. The terrorists can readily find useful idiots to latch on to cryptoterrorist propaganda and parrot its slogans in the name of radical and critical comment. According to these trendy journalists and left-wing politicians, Northern Ireland is a brutally repressive, colonial society directly comparable to Kenya at the time of the Mau-Mau or Cyprus in the days of National Organization of Cypriot Fighters (EOKA). In their eyes, Britain is entirely responsible for causing the conflict in Northern Ireland and continues to be a total failure, with no positive achievements in the province to its credit. With independent journalists like this, the Provisional Sinn Fein hardly needs to conduct a political campaign to change mainland British opinion.

The problem of terrorist political fronts such as the Provisional Sinn Fein is by no means unique to Northern Ireland. Spain, Italy, the Republic of Ireland, and West Germany, for example, have all had to contend with this phenomenon. None of the Continental countries of Western Europe has experienced any terrorist campaign as prolonged and lethal as that of the IRA, yet Spain and West Germany have adopted much tougher measures to limit terrorist propaganda than any introduced in Northern Ireland, and no sensible person seriously believes that these democratic governments are repressive regimes.

The terrorists' political-front organizations, spokespersons, and apologists have set great store on using TV and radio appearances to further all four of the major propaganda efforts listed above. They know that getting their representatives and sympathizers on TV gives them an aura of credibility and power in the eyes of their own constituency, if not among the population in general. It enables them to increase the flow of cash and new recruits into their organization. They use the media to convey and magnify their threats against the community or specific members of it, such as police officers or civil servants.

In view of all this we should hardly be surprised to find that when faced with severe terrorist campaigns several democratic countries have sought to deny the terrorists direct access to the important platform of the broadcast media. For example, Spanish democracy has used very tough measures against the murderous Basque Fatherland and Liberty (ETA) terrorists' propaganda. Madrid introduced a law in 1984 that makes a criminal offense of supporting or praising "the activities typical of a terrorist organization . . . or the deeds or commemorative dates of their members by publishing or broadcasting via the mass media, articles expressing opinion, news reports, graphical illustrations, communiqués, and, in general, by any other form of dissemination." Judges were at one stage even empowered to close down radio stations as an exceptional precautionary measure. In 1976 West Germany brought in the Anti-Constitutional Advocacy Act, making an offense of publicly advocating and/or encouraging others to commit an offense against the stability of the Federal Republic. In the case of Italy's struggle to suppress the Red Brigades, the mass media ultimately decided to set up a voluntary blackout to prevent terrorist manipulation of the mass media. They learned their lesson when the press was shamelessly exploited during the Moro kidnapping.

The closest parallel to the media ban on interviews with Ulster terrorist fronts and spokespersons is the ban in the Irish Republic. In 1972 the Dublin authorities used Section 31 of the republic's 1960 Broadcasting Authority Act to ban the state radio and TV service (RTE) from carrying interviews with Provisional or official IRA representatives and sympathizers. Since October 1976, the ban has been extended to cover interviews or reports of interviews with members of the political wing of the Provisional IRA, the Provisional Sinn Fein, or members of any organization proscribed in Northern Ireland. For instance, in August 1984, a radio interview with a former so-called chief of staff of the IRA, Cathal Goulding, was banned. The Provisional Sinn Fein protests that it is a legal political party in the Republic of Ireland and that it has a legal right to broadcasting time. However, the minister who imposed the ban, Conor Cruise O'Brien, said that the Provisional Sinn Fein was not a legitimate political party but rather a "public relations agency for a murder gang."

Suggesting that the ban on TV and radio interviews will suffice to cut off the terrorists' oxygen supply of publicity would be foolish. As long as they have legal political fronts able to contest elections, for example, they have a ready-made political platform. Whether the British government is planning to curtail the electoral aspect of the IRA's "ballot box and Armalite" strategy remains to be seen. What is already clear is that the Provisionals have suffered a considerable blow to their propaganda effort by the ban on TV and radio interviews. Experience in the Republic of Ireland certainly shows that such a ban can be operated smoothly and efficiently for many years without in any way threatening parliamentary democracy.

Few observers have pointed out that even in a free society no freedom of expression is totally unlimited. Most of us believe, for example, that pornography should be banned from TV and radio. Inviting terrorists on TV to crow about their latest atrocity is the ultimate pornography of violence. Banning them will prevent causing real distress to hundreds of relatives bereaved by terrorist murderers. It will also help to protect the far more basic democratic freedoms of life and liberty by helping to defeat the terrorist murderers who seek to destroy the democratic rights of their fellow citizens.

NOTES

1. Hannah Arendt, *On Revolution* (Harmondsworth: Penguin Books, 1973), p. 19.

2. Alex P. Schmid, *Political Terrorism: A Research Guide to Concepts, Theories, Data Bases and Literature* (Amsterdam: North Holland Publishing Co., 1983), pp. 5–158.

3. Jeffrey Ian Ross and Ted Robert Gurr, "Why Terrorism Subsides: A Comparative Study of Trends and Groups in Canada and the United States." Paper presented to the annual meeting of the American Political Science Association, Chicago, September 1987.

4. Raymond Aron, *Peace and War* (London: Weidenfeld and Nicolson, 1966), p. 170.

5. S. Andreski, "Terror," in Julius Gould and William L. Kolb, eds., *A Dictionary of the Social Sciences* (Glencoe, Ill.: UNESCO and the Free Press, 1964).

6. André Malraux, *La Condition humaine* (Paris: Gallimard, 1946), p. 189.

7. Maurice Tugwell, "Revolutionary Propaganda and Possible Counter-Measures," unpublished Ph.D. thesis, King's College, University of London, 1978.

PART III

Terrorism and the Media

O NE of the principal functions of the police is to deal with crime, and they identify terrorism as such. This attitude is founded in the belief that terrorists are not to be accorded the status of soldiers, which they often seek. Terrorism occurs in a peacetime situation, and related acts are to be treated in the same way murder, wounding, or theft are dealt with under "normal" criminal circumstances. The police have to deal with incidents and are aware that terror campaigns are orchestrated to maximize media coverage. The authorities thus tend to mistrust the media, even with no collusion between terrorists and the media. Mistrust of the establishment and a desire to seek out errors or misdeeds are prevalent among journalists. Given this actual mistrust and a presumed acceptance of the role of a free press in democracies, what is the proper course open to police and media when democracy itself is under attack? Intelligent coexistence is necessary, with each party retaining its independence within its sphere of responsibility.

Terrorists wage physical and propaganda wars that are inseparable. The media inevitably provide the means for terrorists to advance their purposes with a view to subverting the democratic processes through which they are unable to achieve their goals; the media enable them to admit their aims, promise more, frighten the population, and undermine government. The police often argue that this publicity contribute to the growth of misconceptions, fanaticism, and bigotry. Positive media support for police action is felt to be appropriate. Restraint in reporting is urged, despite the recognition that it is difficult to secure in a competitive media environment. Consequently, the option of enforced, legislated restraint is proposed.

The police reasonably indicate on occasion that they do not wish to release all information for fear of jeopardizing public security or police operations. In addition, the terrorists are seeking to undermine public confidence in the security forces; therefore, publication of potentially damaging material requires restraint, although police errors have to be acknowledged and dealt with under law. Liberal democracies accept that the police are accountable under law and to the public via media scrutiny and reporting. The media are felt to have a responsibility not to make allegations that the police are unable to counter because of legal and operational constraints. The police argue that reporting, overdramatization, and the pressure of deadlines should not be overriding features of media coverage. Balanced reporting of terrorism and police activity is urged. The police state frequently that they require the support of society and of the media to counteract terrorism. Police action is not generally perceived as the only solution to the problem; a crucial police requirement is that both media and police be committed to the maintenance of democracy and that their actions reflect that commitment.

CHAPTER 3

The Police, the Media, and the Reporting of Terrorism

Sir John Hermon

DISCUSSION of the media, certainly with the media, is largely a rather emotive subject characterized by mistrust, accusation and counteraccusation, misunderstanding, sometimes dogmatic assertions, and mutual wariness. All these ingredients and more are readily recognized.

Additionally, the general nature of the media, including methods of portrayal by sections of it, is such that one must always exercise considerable caution and awareness of its influence and power. Specifically within the Northern Ireland context in commenting on issues, events, or the actions of individuals or groups, inherent dangers and sensitivities preclude any comment that is remotely capable of being manipulated or distorted via the media. Ill-chosen words, duly exploited, can have devastating repercussions within the community.

Exploitation by the media is not, of course, a new phenomenon. More than a century ago, so the story goes, President Lincoln was asked if he thought the press reliable. The president pondered for a moment and replied: "Yes, I reckon the press are reliable. They lie; and then they re-lie. They are nothing if not reliable." A journalist, assessing the establishment, would no doubt tell the story the other way around:

Therefore, our credentials ought to be put on the table. Stating clearly a fundamental belief in a free press, by which is meant the media as a whole, is not trite or superfluous merely because it has been asserted so often by so many others. This is not lip service. The media constitute an indispensable factor in the framework of our democracy. That belief certainly is the only basis or context on which we would proceed to discuss the difficulties and problems arising from the practice of the principle, difficulties and problems existing in an environment in which democracy is under threat and the various elements—governments, politicians, police forces, and the media, to mention but a few—have had difficult judgments and decisions to make.

Sensible, informed communication has to be the basis of the relationship between the police and the news media. It may be described as intelligent coexistence rather than as compromising cohabitation. This relationship is essential if the police are to discharge fully their obligation of accountability to the public they serve. The police have several statutory and other very real accountabilities—to the law through the courts, to Parliament, to the Director of Public Prosecutions, to the Police Authority, to the Police Complaints Authority, and to Her Majesty's Inspector of Constabulary. Each of these is a vital part of the scheme of things. Even though the accountability is nonstatutory, police answerability to the news media is also very real and very, very powerful. Certainly, in Northern Ireland the police operate unremittingly under the microscope of media interest and scrutiny. Our policies, our attitudes, and our actions are subjected to intense and unceasing media attention locally, nationally, and internationally. That statement is not a complaint but simply a fact. It also constitutes a pressure with which we have had to learn to cope professionally.

We cannot deviate from that straight line on either side of which is the complex jungle that would readily smother those forces of impartiality, integrity, and professionalism so fundamental to successful and improved policing of the community. We must always be sensitive, alert, and more clever than those who seek to further disorder and terrorism if we are to avoid the trap of alienating the community in whose midst the terrorist resides.

That concept perhaps brings us naturally to the subject of terrorism, the media, the inevitable difficulties for all of us, and the questions that exercise our minds.

In Northern Ireland, terrorist organizations, principally but not solely Sinn Fein and the Provisional IRA, are waging two wars: on the one hand, the physical war of death and destruction, and on the other hand, the propaganda war. Although we separate these to make a point, they are in fact inseparable. One nourishes and sustains the other. They constitute one war. In innumerable instances in the past and doubtless more to follow, terrorist outrages have been planned and timed so as to exploit the media to its absolute limits and to attract maximum publicity. The propaganda element is of crucial importance to the terrorist, who recognizes how vital publicity is to sustain and advance the criminal purpose. The terrorist shows no hesitation or lack of skill in exploiting the benefits of democracy—in this case an open press—in order to subvert democracy. What is democracy's answer to be to this abuse of its own processes?

In Northern Ireland, terrorist organizations and their spurious political fronts have, in the face of community rejection, ruthlessly and persistently used the media to admit murder, to justify murder, to threaten murder, to intimidate the whole community and sections of it, to try to undermine the lawfully constituted authority, to poison people's minds, and so to perpetuate and reinforce the alienation, the bigotry, the hatred, the ignorance, and the fanaticism on which their campaign of violence is based.

Is this freedom accorded to the terrorists a necessary price to pay in defense of democracy itself? Should the media adopt the neutral stance of mere spectators of the democratic process under threat as distinct from being active, discerning, concerned participants in the process, or do they do their disparate, imperfect best to exercise judgment, including self-imposed partial censorship?

Given the highly competitive nature of the media, with their cutthroat grabbing for circulation figures and audiences, can we at all realistically expect the media to exercise any cohesive restraint or reasonable degree of responsibility in accepting the newsiness of terrorism, or should the state, with its ultimate responsibility, enter the debate decisively and say, "No, the general democratic good demands that terrorist criminals not have the freedom to disseminate their criminal propaganda"?

These questions are not just philosophically interesting, abstract, or merely academic; in Northern Ireland they impinge on the daily lives of people, on the quality of their lives, and indeed on life itself. We might consider a comment posed by one Royal Ulster Constabulary (RUC) divisional commander, "Would a rapist in Hampshire or a burglar in Berkshire be accorded the freedom through the media to justify rape and burglary and be allowed to threaten more of the same?"

National security is currently a contentious issue in Northern Ireland and on the mainland. Obviously, security is a matter of vital importance to the police and the army in the province. It is literally a matter of life and death for them—their lives and the lives of the people who desperately seek and need their protection. Security is not a matter of secrecy for the sake of secrecy itself. Many lives have been saved and the stability of the province protected through the necessary existence of the secrecy attached to security matters. The freedom of the media is not and surely cannot be an absolute freedom. It is circumscribed by law in various respects, for example, by the law of libel in safeguarding a person's good reputation. The safeguarding of life is surely an overwhelming necessary protection that imposes legitimate limitations and responsibilities on the media in reporting the conduct of terrorism and the state's response to it.

A very genuine, definite public interest is at stake. We cannot accept a view that so-called investigative journalism has no bounds at all, that it can ignore to any degree the consequences of exposure, or that it can choose to adopt an overtly loose or ill-considered interpretation of the "public interest" publication criterion.

Part of the strategy of terrorist organizations in Northern Ireland is to erode public confidence in and support for the police and the army, to undermine their morale and effectiveness, and to portray them as thugs in uniform and oppressors brutally enforcing a discredited system. The community thus faces a barrage of such propaganda through the media from the terrorist organizations, their front organizations, and fellow travelers. The virulence of their vocabulary has done some damage to the English language, not to mention the damage to people's minds. Alongside this propaganda, criticism of and allegations against the security forces from public figures and elements of the media who, while themselves abjuring and condemning violence, unjustly abuse the security forces in immoderate language that sometimes echoes that of the terrorist. Of course, the security forces do make mistakes; they are not immune to imperfect judgments and behavior, nor do they not accept and attempt to learn from justified criticism of their action. However, we must balance very carefully and responsibly public criticism of the police or any against the overall and long-term public good. The terrorist undoubtedly draws comfort and confirmation from these "respectable" sources of condemnation of the security forces.

We should emphasize that the police and the army in Northern Ireland are not asking to be exempt from criticism, for a convenient blind eye to be turned to wrongdoing, for freedom to operate outside the law without too many, or any, questions being asked, or for a license to preach one thing and to practice another according to our choosing. They ask none of these things. They are accountable, but the terrorist has no such accountability.

Quite often the most outrageous allegations can be publicized—indeed sensationalized—by the media, and quite often the police and the army, for good reasons, are not able to respond adequately, or at all, at the time. Over the years, some elements of the media and some individual journalists have not lived up to that degree of judgment, honesty, fairness, responsibility, and integrity that they themselves so insistently demand of the security forces. As a result, damage has unfairly been inflicted on the police and the army as organizations, and on individuals within those organizations. The security forces are frequently asked to examine their actions and attitudes. Perhaps some conscience-searching would not be out of place by some sections or people within the media, or does a "good" story transcend all other considerations? Are the police and the army fair game for anything and everything? Are the overriding imperatives simply deadlines to be met and space to be filled?

The police are a part of the community. They do not come from Mars or emanate from somewhere in outer space. They have homes, families, and interests in the community and a stake in it as citizens. They are therefore interested in the total welfare of their community, which includes how Northern Ireland is portrayed at home and abroad because, among other things, it has an effect on their economic livelihoods. Indisputably, Northern Ireland is afflicted by a degree of abnormality, terrible and shocking events occur there, and despicable people commit atrocious crimes. Nevertheless, normality prevails there, much that is good and admirable happens, decency abounds, and good people make up the vast majority, regardless of their religion or politics. Are these aspects of truth sufficiently portrayed? Do the media too often unintentionally or unthinkingly succumb to the temptation of the graffiti, the destruction, the divisions, the differences, the violence of the vocabulary, all of which make "good" pictures and "good" copy? Is the image portrayed of Northern Ireland here and around the world fair and fully in accord with reality?

Even allowing for pride and prejudice in the matter of our native province, we are bound to say that many visitors who come to Northern Ireland discover a considerable and pleasing disparity between the actual experience and the image previously established in their hands through the media. The terrorist has a strong vested interest in conveying abnormality and in the projection of a distorted picture. The media have a heavy responsibility not to assist unthinkingly in that objective.

The crucial role of a responsible free press in the democratic scheme of things is accepted. The observations made are not to be taken as altering or detracting from that stance. They do not represent any sense of sourness or grievance. The difficulties facing journalists in reporting the suffering of a divided community under assault from various terrorist organizations are acknowledged. The best of journalism is in the broad middle ground trying to do a fair, decent, and honest job in stressful circumstances. In that respect, journalism and policing have a strong affinity.

Pointed questions are asked, however, because they relate to real issues. If criticism is implied or expressed, then the balance could not be better expressed than in another question: Who could gainsay or forget the power or the poignancy of the images brought to us and to the whole world by the news media out of Enniskillen in 1987? Out of the coverage of that tragedy by the media came dignity, compassion, hope, and a powerful indictment of terrorism. In 1986 extreme loyalist elements directed their pernicious acts of intimidation, physical abuse, petrol bomb attacks, criminal damage, and arson attacks on Catholic homes, schools, places of worship, and businesses, on moderate Protestant loyalists, or politicians, and, of course, on such a wide scale on the homes of police officers and their families. Who could doubt that the media portrayal of that politically motivated campaign was an important factor in creating the public revulsion and pressure that led to a virtual cessation of that form of attack? Less dramatically, more routinely, but still most importantly, daily the news media publicize the many ordinary aspects of policing as well as our appeals for information about terrorist crimes.

All that said, serious questions do remain to be examined. We do not ask for any special indulgence that compromises the role of the media or creates for the police a favored status, regardless of competence, professionalism, or behavior. We accept completely that the police must have the capability to speak articulately for themselves, to defend themselves robustly when wronged, and most of all to account for themselves publicly without seeking refuge in spurious secrecy or arrogantly regarding themselves as above inquiry or question.

However, the police are entitled to ask for support in combating terrorism, for understanding of the role of the police, and for media responsibility in reporting their affairs and the most difficult and dangerous matters with which they have to deal. The police do not and must not stand alone. The police and the media have their respective roles and responsibilities. The police have no desire whatsoever to control the media, nor will the media dictate police business. This independence is right and healthy. Nevertheless, both are part of the same democratic process and belief, and the basis for any discussion is the fact that they both should and indeed must have a commitment to its preservation. In that, surely they do not stand apart, nor can they afford the luxury of selfishly or narrowly asserting their own particular rights to the detriment of the common good.

PART IV

The U.S. Perspective

IN THE UNITED STATES, coverage of terrorist incidents, particularly by television, may be intensive. Involvement of the media provides the same questions on each occasion: Are the networks used by the terrorists? Do they damage U.S. interests by excessive coverage that weakens the government's ability to deal with the crisis? Do network "stars" across the line separating journalism from diplomacy? To what degree does competition among the networks affect the story?

Following the hijacking of Trans World Airlines Flight 847 in 1985, during a debate on the role of television in coverage of terrorism, Prime Minister Thatcher urged news organizations to restrain their coverage of terrorism and stated that television should "find ways to starve terrorists . . . of the oxygen of publicity." Attorney General Edwin Meese stated that the U.S. government might ask news organizations to adopt a code of restraint and that broadcasters might be asked to agree to "some principles reduced to writing." The options of voluntary restraint or governmental control were clearly raised.

Following the TWA incident, a number of U.S. news organizations, including United Press International (UPI), the *Chicago Sun-Times,* and the Columbia Broadcasting System (CBS), independently drafted guidelines for the coverage of terrorist incidents and hostage-taking. These agencies developed policies to the effect that they would avoid providing an excessive platform for terrorists, that they would not provide live coverage of terrorism, and that coverage would not sensationalize a story beyond the fact of its being sensational. The guidelines attempt to shape responsible coverage while recognizing that no automatic rules can be made for coverage of incidents where the facts and circumstances inevitably vary.

The view that television is the terrorists' ultimate tool implies that the granting of airtime to terrorists and to the events they stage-manage is akin to assisting them to secure sympathy and support. However, the force of this argument is rejected by many, who take the view that television is a feature of modern life that simply reflects events as they unfold. The public expects to be informed through proper coverage of these events and accepts that this coverage may on occasion be inconvenient, intrusive, or harmful.

Some argue that the U.S. government also stage-manages coverage to affect the outcome of an incident or to send signals to groups involved. The criticism has been made that media reports on U.S. military movements provide information that might be useful to terrorists. However, virtually all information regarding military and diplomatic moves comes from government officials who provide it on the understanding that it is to be revealed. This policy ensures that the potential target group is aware of the possibility of military intervention in reaction to their activities.

The media argue that extensive coverage need not necessarily further terrorist aims or unduly alarm the public and that the nature of the coverage may be a more important factor. To follow exclusively the government line and interpretation opens the media to the charge of being the stooge and propaganda tool of the government. Journalists and broadcasters are seen to embrace a philosophy that assumes a reality that they are to reflect accurately and recapture in all its detail so that an objective representation of the real world is presented. In practice, however, reality is filtered through the editing of news content. Broadcast networks keep an eye on the ratings of their competitors and on the changing tastes of the audience. The dramatic visual effects of terrorism are perfectly suited for television. The media pursue their own self-interest and seek to sell a story effectively. Media personnel note that they face a genuine dilemma in balancing censorship and the public's right to know and that, in practice, restraints are already in place. For instance, the U.S. press did not report that one hostage on Flight 847 was a member of the National Security Agency, which would have endangered him.

The debate on these questions is inevitably influenced by the overall political and legal context within which the U.S. media operate. The structure of U.S. media—decentralized, commercial, and competitive—affects the way news is reported. The U.S. media are not subject to the type of legal constraints that exist in many European countries; they have no equivalent of the British D-Notice system, for example. This situation is in part a function of the First Amendment to the U.S. Constitution, which guarantees freedom of the press. However, the activity of the U.S. media is not without limits. Even in routine situations, government seeks to influence news coverage as a matter of course and is effective to varying degrees. Also, the media may not report without consequences; organizations may be sued through the courts for damages resulting from their news coverage. In emergency situations, a stronger tradition of U.S. government intervention exists; for example, President Lincoln took rigorous measures against Confederate newspaper editors during the Civil War. Extraordinary powers are available under conditions of martial law, through which government control of the media would be substantial; such powers would possibly be invoked should terrorist incidents proliferate in the United States.

However, given the generally unrestricted media environment within the United States, the sometimes contradictory demands for security and the maintenance of democratic values may be particularly acute. The crucial issue is one of balance, of seeking to ensure that journalists share and apply the ethics and basic values of the liberal democratic society in which they work. Only this outlook can enable media-generated guidelines to operate effectively. Such a system will inevitably be imperfect and violations will occur, but the consensus within the U.S. media remains that this price is worthwhile for operating within a democratic society.

Critics of U.S. media behavior take issue with the argument of its representatives that it effectively protects democracy. Commercial pressures—for example, to secure advertising—generate a predisposition to present news in a sensational way. Evidence of a more responsible attitude following criticism of media coverage of the TWA hijacking is felt to be inadequate. The U.S. military authorities challenge the view that information on counterterrorist preparations is released by government sources; press coverage is said to involve speculation. Information released as background may be published because of competition between national and local media, the latter releasing details in order to compete successfully with national outlets, which in turn follow this lead once a story has broken. The view that the media behave responsibly (apart from an irresponsible minority) is questioned; the tendency of the media to follow up and elaborate on items first released by maverick reporters indicates that responsibility breaks down once an item is released into the public domain. Although the credibility of unreliable reporters may be undermined over time, the damage they can cause in the meantime may be considerable. Many observers feel that the general standards of media reporting and the exercise of restraint are inadequate.

In countering these criticisms, we can observe that the peculiarities of the U.S. media system reflect the nature of the society in which it operates. The society has been termed competitive and subject to conflict and high levels of tension. As such it is a reflection of American wishes on how they wish their society to function. Similarly, the U.S. media, with their high level of investigative excellence, high profile, and independence, receive a generally positive reception within U.S. society. Introducing and applying agreed ethics to govern the reporting of terrorism need not undermine this general state of affairs. A balance between security and democratic values may be struck. The nature of this balance may differ in different countries, a truism demonstrated by the case of the United States.

CHAPTER 4

Media Coverage of Political Terrorism and the First Amendment: Reconciling the Public's Right to Know with Public Order

John E. Finn

THE TOPIC is large and unwieldy: the First Amendment and media coverage of political terrorism. Such discussions commonly proceed fairly quickly to an examination of possible restraints upon media coverage and then to whether those restraints should be imposed by governmental authorities or should instead be voluntarily adopted by a responsible and disciplined press. The former proposal immediately and properly evokes fears of censorship, the latter doubts about utility and feasibility.

These questions are important and contentious. For now, however, they are premature. They rest upon a set of assumptions that the literature on terrorism too easily takes for granted. Foremost among these unexamined assumptions is the fairly routine claim that the media somehow promote terrorism, either as an active, gullible, or naive partner or by providing an irresistible forum for publicity and propaganda. We are all familiar with claims about the symbiotic nature of the relationship between the media and terrorism: violence sells and violence is newsworthy; terrorism is theater and terrorism entertains.

Freedom of speech and association hold a privileged constitutional position in democratic states. This position does not mean, as some seem to argue, that freedom of speech is an absolute and inviolable value. As discussed later in this chapter, the constitutions of most democratic states contemplate times when commitment to civil liberties must be sacrificed in the name of security. The most difficult issues terrorism raises in democratic states are not questions of physical integrity but rather of spiritual integrity, of the strength of our commitment to two or more positive values that appear irreconcilable. The apparent conflict is between our commitment to unhindered public discourse and the need for public security. This conflict is only one aspect of a much larger conflict between security and democratic aspiration. It does mean, however, that in a constitutional democracy those who advocate the need for and the legality of media restraints, whether voluntary or mandatory, as do those who oppose them, have an obligation first to examine those assumptions and the empirical claim upon which they rest.

A series of straightforward but thoroughly contentious questions must be examined. Answers to these questions are an essential precondition to an intelligent discussion of whether the media in constitutional states should voluntarily adopt certain restraints or whether governmental authorities should impose certain constraints on media coverage of terrorism. A minimum set of concerns exists that the advocates of restraints must satisfy if they are to make a persuasive case for their position. The concerns are specified without supposing that they can or cannot be satisfied. Opponents of media regulation should be required to address a similar set of questions.

MEDIA COVERAGE AND THE FREQUENCY OF TERRORIST EVENTS

First we need to establish precisely what the relationship, if any, is between aggressive media coverage of terrorist spectaculars and terrorist incidents. In other words, does media coverage influence terrorism and, if so, how? In addressing this question, we must be careful to distinguish between two distinct issues. The first is a matter of frequency. Proponents of restraints typically claim that media coverage of political violence encourages additional terrorist acts. Commonly known as the "contagion effect," the argument proposes that media coverage of terrorism inspires repetition in the group that undertook the violent act and subsequently profited from the coverage, as well as imitation and emulation by other groups. In the former case, media coverage "reinforces the terrorists' sense of power and . . . may contribute significantly to the prolonging of the incident or to an increase in its serious consequences."[1] Imitation and emulation by other groups are a consequence because they learn that terrorism is a powerful currency with which to purchase publicity. Moreover, excessive media coverage may teach in other, more direct ways, perhaps by providing these groups with tactical or strategic information that they can later use to advantage.

The contagion effects of terrorism have been the subject of rigorous research, much of which has shown that it "is a demonstrably contagious phenomenon."[2] However, these findings should be interpreted carefully. The media may play an important structural role in determining the highly imitative character of terrorism, a point addressed below, but the larger and more important case that media coverage has substantially increased the frequency of terrorist incidents is very difficult to make, at least as measured by absolute increases in political violence. Indeed, the last few years have seen much talk about how the frequency of terrorist incidents has seemed to decrease recently. The question arises as to what may have caused this recession in the economy of violence. Of course, some measure other than absolute increases in violence could be chosen for all sorts of good reasons, not least of which is the unreliability of such data, but the proponents of media restraints have yet to suggest what that other measure should be or why it is more appropriate than others.

Another possibility is that the prospect of publicity through media coverage serves to encourage opposition groups to employ violence as a tool for political change, as opposed to less violent and hence less newsworthy methods of political action. In this case, the issue is less one of distributional frequency than of proclivity; media coverage lowers the threshold. Much interesting work needs to be done here. Unfortunately, however, the literature on decision-making within terrorist organizations is still in its infancy.[3] We cannot yet conclude that excessive media coverage acts as an incentive in the strategic choices terrorist organizations make.

The second question is not of frequency but of form. Whatever the effects of media coverage on the frequency or distribution of terrorism, the media—in particular, the electronic media—might affect the specific forms that terrorism takes. Terrorism often appears faddish. Diplomatic and commercial kidnappings were especially common in Latin America in the 1960s and 1970s. Aircraft hijackings and car bombings were frequent throughout the 1970s; hostage-taking characterized the 1980s.

As indicated earlier, scholarly research demonstrates the imitative character of political terrorism, and undoubtedly the media glamorization of spectacular terrorist acts helps make such imitation possible. No doubt terrorist organizations learn in much the same ways that other organizations do. Nevertheless, this process is hardly novel and not unique to terrorism. The subject has bedeviled criminology for decades. All that can be said is that the media *may* influence the form and specific character of terrorist strategy—quite a different claim and a much weaker one than the argument that media coverage actually encourages or promotes terrorism. The first claim about the relationship between the media and political terrorism, if it can be demonstrated, might support restraints upon media coverage. The second claim is much less certain a foundation.

MEDIA INVOLVEMENT IN TERRORIST INCIDENTS

A second set of issues involves not so much the relationship between media coverage and the frequency of terrorism as the effects of coverage during an ongoing terrorist incident. Critics often complain that the media have improperly interfered during the course of an incident, perhaps by broadcasting sensitive information or by involving themselves in negotiations. This charge is not frivolous, but again we must take care to distinguish between things that are not alike.

On one level, media coverage of terrorist incidents necessarily affects how the participants act. Something very much like the Heisenberg uncertainty principle operates in such circumstances, as observation remakes and changes what is observed. (Some version of this truth explains much of the faddish character of terrorist violence. Hijackings lose their glamor and interest through repeated exposure and must then be replaced with some other, novel form of violence.) Of course, the media can be cautioned not to sensationalize, but how this influence can be avoided without an expansive form of censorship is unclear. Why censorship would be appropriate for this reason alone is also not certain. That the mere presence of the media affects the conduct of terrorist incidents is one claim, and that media presence *necessarily* hampers the successful resolution of such incidents is quite another claim. Instances can be recalled in which the media's presence caused problems, but at times it has helped as well.

The task, then, is to identify with greater precision the areas in which media involvement has been troublesome and, if they are thought to be exigent, to tailor restraints to just those situations. Two areas are of particular concern here. In some cases, the media have publicized sensitive information and intelligence that may have handicapped the efforts of authorities to cope with terrorist incidents, especially hijackings and other hostage situations. In what is perhaps the most serious case, radio broadcasts alerted the hijackers of a Lufthansa jet that the plane's captain was transmitting information to ground authorities. The hijackers subsequently killed the captain. Americans may also recall the Hanafi Muslim case, in which radio and television broadcasters went so far as to conduct live interviews with the Hanafis. Chapter 5 details the media's involvement in the 1985 hijacking of TWA Flight 847; after the incident ended, the London *Times* wrote that "the behavior of the American television crews and companies was a disgrace." Excessive television coverage, including, as in this case, stage-managed news conferences with some of the hostages, may act as an incentive to terrorists to prolong the incident and may thus hinder the efforts of governmental authorities to resolve it.

These incidents clearly indicate the need for discretion and discipline in how the media actually cover terrorist incidents. Once again, however, whether anything more is required here than what the media typically demand of themselves in reporting nonterroristic hostage situations is not clear. The appeal must be to the professional integrity of journalists; respect for those professional values, coupled with cooperation between authorities and media representatives, does more to avoid difficulties of the sort outlined than would legal regulation. Mandatory restraints inevitably invite deliberate violation, especially among what is commonly called the popular press. They promote an environment of continued antagonism between the press and security officials. The antagonism would be most unfortunate for, as indicated before, the presence of the press in such cases is not necessarily negative. Moreover, instances of cooperation occur. Several American police departments, including that of New York City, as well as the FBI, now invite media representatives to training sessions for hostage negotiators.

Another point should not be ignored. Security forces often claim, with good reason, that they have learned over time how best to cope with terrorist situations and that their sophistication increases with experience. American media representatives now make a similar claim that should not be dismissed out of hand. With experience, the press came to honor requests for restraint in the reporting of criminal kidnap cases. The press also chose not to report that one of the hostages on TWA Flight 847 was a member of the National Security Agency.

MEDIA RESTRAINTS, THE FIRST AMENDMENT, AND CIVIL LIBERTIES

The foregoing leaves open the question of support for opposition to legal restraints upon media coverage of political terrorism. The imposition of restraints without first specifying the reasons why they are necessary and under what conditions they are tolerable is, however, to be opposed. The proponents of restraints have not yet satisfied these requirements. The burden of such justification is a heavy one. Some will respond that such a burden is too stringent and that it substantially underestimates the threat terrorism poses for democratic states and the role the media play in making that threat effective.

As indicated earlier, however, the threat that terrorism poses for democratic societies is greatly overstated, notwithstanding repeated warnings in scholarly and popular literature that democratic states are especially and unusually vulnerable to political terrorism. Much of that vulnerability is attributed to the freedom such states guarantee the media. Nevertheless, the cases in which terrorists have posed a truly substantial threat to the physical integrity of Western democracies are in truth quite infrequent, if indeed they have happened at all.[4]

Far more common and far more troublesome are the hazards terrorism poses to the spiritual integrity of Western democracies and to their commitment to democratic and constitutional principles. Widespread terrorism, like other forms of political violence, typically evokes claims in democracies that we cannot adequately protect ourselves if we strictly adhere to constitutional limitations upon governmental power, limitations we freely adopted in less troublesome times. Claims of this sort have led many to conclude that the real danger is not terrorism but rather how we choose to respond to it. Indeed, one prominent student of terrorism has concluded that the "consequences of terrorism have a great deal to do with the limits each society imposes on the civil liberties of its citizenry to secure its survival,"[5] and Paul Wilkinson warns that "the real danger of resorting to sledgehammer methods to cope with the relatively low intensities of political violence . . . in most Western countries is that they would extinguish democracy in the name of security."[6] This concern, above all others, counsels caution in the legal regulation of media coverage of terrorism. However, these concerns constitute just one aspect of the larger problem.

These fears should not be dismissed; indeed, they are quite real and terribly important. Nevertheless, they tend to proceed at a level of generality not unlike claims about how the media promotes terrorism, and for this reason, as well as some others, they are just as unsatisfactory. As Martha Crenshaw has noted, remarkably few studies "document the concrete effects of policies against terrorism on individual freedoms."[7] Only a few studies describe the content of antiterrorist policies in any detail, and we know even less about the operation and implementation of antiterrorist legislation.[8] That neglect is really quite surprising, for every major Western democracy has either proposed or enacted special antiterrorist legislation to respond to terrorism. In the Republic of Ireland and in Northern Ireland in the United Kingdom, for example, the police possess expansive powers of arrest and detention, and in both states special courts are charged with jurisdiction over terrorist offenses. These courts sit without juries and operate under substantially relaxed rules of procedure and evidence. The constitutions of Italy and the Federal Republic of Germany explicitly prohibit special courts, but both countries have enacted legislation that grants authorities sweeping powers of arrest and detention. France, Canada, the Netherlands, Denmark, and Belgium have all enacted antiterrorist legislation as well. Frequently these efforts include restrictions on press coverage of terrorist incidents. Section 3(1) (a) of the Canadian War Measures Act, for instance, provides that the governor in council may issue regulations concerning "censorship and the control and suppression of publications, writings, maps, plans, photographs, communications and the means of communication."

Perhaps the most notable example is Section 31 of the 1960 Broadcasting Authority Act in the Republic of Ireland. Acting under this section in 1972, then Minister of Posts and Telegraphs Conor Cruise O'Brien banned state radio and television networks from broadcasting interviews with Irish Republican Army officials or known sympathizers. In 1976 the government expanded the prohibition to include interviews with members of Sinn Fein (the political counterpart of the IRA) or with members of any organization proscribed under the Northern Ireland Emergency Provisions Act of 1973. Sinn Fein is a legal political party in Britain and routinely runs candidates in general elections in Northern Ireland.

Concerns have been expressed in Great Britain as well. Prime Minister Thatcher has spoken repeatedly about the media's responsibility to deprive terrorists of the "oxygen of publicity," and of late the D-Notice system has received renewed criticism. Moreover, critics of the Prevention of Terrorism Act of 1976 have charged that Section 10, which creates a number of criminal offenses that generally concern "support" for terrorist organizations, has led the British media to decline to televise some documentaries on the Northern Irish problem for fear that they might "encourage support" for the IRA and other banned organizations. In the summer of 1980, for example, the BBC refused to televise two documentaries presented by the British Film Institute because they "lacked balance."

More recently, BBC broadcast journalists went on strike after the BBC's

Board of Governors, under pressure from the home secretary, overruled management's decision to televise a documentary on Northern Ireland, *Real Lives: At the Edge of the Union,* because it featured interviews with Martin McGuinness of Sinn Fein and Gregory Campbell of the Democratic Unionist Party. Both men held elective office.

Claims are frequently made that such problems are not possible in the United States because the First Amendment absolutely prohibits governmental regulation of the news media and their coverage of terrorism. Although individual justices have insisted that the First Amendment absolutely prohibits governmental restraints upon the media, that position does not accurately reflect First Amendment jurisprudence. President Lincoln took rigorous measures against certain editors of Confederate newspapers during the Civil War. As recently as 1971, a probable majority of the justices of the Supreme Court, although they could not agree upon a common opinion, could agree in the Pentagon Papers case[9] that in extraordinary circumstances, such as those occasioned by war or some other emergency, governmental restrictions upon the media might be warranted under some notion of constitutional necessity.

In 1971 the *New York Times* and the *Washington Post* gained access to stolen copies of the Pentagon Papers, a governmental study of American policy decisions in Vietnam. After the newspapers began to publish excerpts of the material, the Department of Justice sought federal injunctions against further publication. One federal court granted a temporary injunction, and a second refused to issue one. The Supreme Court accepted the case, heard oral arguments, and issued an opinion just four days later.

In his concurring opinion, Justice William Brennan wrote:

> Our cases . . . have indicated that there is a single, extremely narrow class of cases in which the First Amendment's ban on prior judicial restraint may be overridden. . . . Such cases may arise only when the Nation is ''at war,'' . . . during which times ''no one would question but that a government might prevent actual obstruction to its recruiting service or the publication of the sailing dates of transports or the number and location of troops.''

Likewise, Justice Harry Blackmun agreed in dissent that ''the First Amendment, after all, is only one part of an entire Constitution. . . . First Amendment absolutism has never commanded a majority of this Court.''[10]

The First Amendment notwithstanding, then, governmental restraints upon the media may be both necessary and constitutionally permissible in a crisis of sufficient severity. The burden of justification is a heavy one, however, and as suggested earlier the proponents of mandatory restraints have yet to produce anything like the evidence necessary to make the case persuasive.

The case is strong enough, however, to warrant voluntary self-regulation. Many people have offered numerous proposals that are quite interesting and generally thoughtful, but they do not substantially improve upon or differ from those presented in the Report of the Task Force on Disorders and

Terrorism (1976). Among the more prominent proposals are the following:

1. Limitations on interviews during hostage incidents
2. Delays upon the release of inflammatory or sensitive information
3. Minimum intrusiveness in the course of terrorist incidents
4. Balanced and noninflammatory coverage of such incidents

Several news organizations have promulgated their own standards. These rules often coincide with the recommendations of the task force, but differences exist as well. The best known of these guidelines are those of the CBS News Division (see appendix 8).[11] These too call for balanced coverage, avoiding "the use of inflammatory catchwords or phrases," and avoiding the provision of "an excessive platform for the terrorist/kidnapper."

Occasionally, some media representatives oppose even self-regulation; they claim that it is only a more subtle form of censorship. At best, this claim is spurious. Although proposals for self-regulation vary in particulars, all essentially amount to little more than exhortations to practice responsible and balanced reporting. They appeal, in other words, to the standards of ethical and responsible behavior that inhere in journalism as an honorable profession.

Skeptics will deny that such values exist, and nothing written here is likely to disabuse them of their doubt. Realists will insist that the competitive structure of the news industry, at least as it functions in the United States, forces even the most responsible of news organizations and journalists to compromise those values. If so, such compromise is a cost of our commitment to democratic values. Democracy *is* a messy business. Our commitment to it and to the protection of civil liberties is often inconvenient, inefficient, annoying, and profoundly costly.

SOME CONCLUDING THOUGHTS

As mentioned in the introductory remarks, the topic—reconciling the public's right to know in cases of terrorism with the demands of public security—is large and unwieldy. The topic is also but a specific example of a much larger and older problem: what the framers of the American Constitution called "good government" can be established upon the basis of reason and deliberation or, in the words of Edmond Cahn, upon the promise "that persuasion and free assent can triumph over brute force and build the foundations of a happier commonwealth."[12] The widespread use of political terrorism in a democratic state casts doubt upon and challenges that promise, but failure to respond to terrorism in a fashion consistent with democratic ideals calls into question our commitment to those ideals and in that respect challenges our very identity.

The larger problem, then, is one of conflicting objectives. Responding to terrorism exposes a conflict between our need for survival, the most urgent objective, and our commitment to democracy, our highest purpose. In this one respect, the oft-repeated charge that democratic societies are especially susceptible to terrorism contains an element of truth. However, this claim obscures as much as it illuminates. The founders of constitutional democracies are generally aware of the historic frailty of such communities, and they typically include provisions in their constitutions that acknowledge the occasional necessity for expansive powers of self-defense. Article I, Section 9 of the U.S. Constitution authorizes suspension of the writ of habeas corpus in cases of "rebellion or invasion" and when "the public safety may require it." Section 8 empowers Congress to declare war and raise armies and to provide militia to suppress insurrections, and we have already seen that First Amendment guarantees are not absolute. Among the less explicit provisions for crisis government are Article II, which provides that executive power is vested in the president, and Section 3 of the same article, which requires that the president faithfully execute the laws.

European constitutions are generally more precise. The Irish Constitution of 1937, for example, expressly authorizes special emergency laws and sanctions the creation of emergency courts. Moreover, Article 28(3) states:

> Nothing in this Constitution shall be invoked to invalidate any law enacted by the legislature which is expressly to be for the purpose of securing the public safety and the preservation of the State in time of war or armed rebellion.

The Basic Law of the Federal Republic of Germany sets forth in Article 115 and various other provisions a detailed catalog of procedures the German government must follow in declaring and coping with states of emergency. In direct contrast to the Irish Constitution, Article 101 of the Basic Law prohibits extraordinary courts. An amendment, Article 155g, further provides that the "constitutional status and the exercise of the constitutional functions [of the Federal Constitutional Court] must not be impaired."

Most democratic states, then, have constitutionally sanctioned powers of emergency. Therefore, attributing the vulnerability of democratic states to political terrorism to an imagined constitutional incapacity is a gross mistake. The means to protect ourselves against the physical threat exist; only resolution wards off the greater threat to our identity.

NOTES

1. Grant Wardlaw, *Political Terrorism: Theory, Tactic, and Countermeasures* (Cambridge: Cambridge University Press, 1982), p. 77.

2. Martha Crenshaw, ed., *Terrorism, Legitimacy, and Power: The Consequences of Political Violence* (Middletown, Conn.: Wesleyan University Press, 1983), p. 17. See also Manus I. Midlarsky, Martha Crenshaw, and Fumihiko Yoshida, "Why Violence Spreads: The Contagion of International Terrorism," *International Studies Quarterly* 24 (1980): 262.

3. See, for example, Kent Layne Oots, *A Political Organization Approach to Transnational Terrorism* (Westport, Conn.: Greenwood Press, 1986).

4. See, for example, Yehezkel Dror, "Terrorism as a Challenge to the Democratic Capacity to Govern," in Martha Crenshaw, ed., *Terrorism, Legitimacy, and Power.* One might argue about Uruguay.

5. Irving Louis Horowitz, "The Routinization of Terrorism and Its Unanticipated Conse-

quences," in Martha Crenshaw, ed., *Terrorism, Legitimacy, and Power*, p. 50. See also Irving Louis Horowitz, "Can Democracy Cope with Terrorism?" *Civil Liberties Review* 4 (1977): 29.

6. Paul Wilkinson, *Terrorism and the Liberal State*, 2d ed. (New York: New York University Press, 1986), pp. 38–50.

7. Crenshaw, *Terrorism, Legitimacy, and Power*, p. 14.

8. There are exceptions. See, for example, Ronald D. Crelinsten, Danielle Laberge-Altmjed, and Dennis Szabo, eds., *Terrorism and Criminal Justice* (Lexington, Mass.: D.C. Heath, 1978); Christopher Hewitt, *The Effectiveness of Antiterrorist Policies* (New York: University Press of America, 1984); Yonah Alexander and Allan S. Nanes, eds., *Legislative Responses to Terrorism* (Boston: Martinus Nijhoff Publishers, 1986); and Kevin Boyle, Thomas Hadden, and Paddy Hillyard, *Ten Years On: The Legal Control of Political Violence* (Nottingham: Russell Press, 1980).

9. *New York Times* v. *United States*, 403 U.S. 713 (1971). See also *Near* v. *Minnesota*, 283 U.S. 697 (1931).

10. "The Pentagon Papers Case," *New York Times company* v. *U.S.*, 403 U.S. 713 (1971).

11. These are discussed and reprinted in Wardlow, *Political Terrorism*, pp. 193–194.

12. Edmond Cahn, "The Consumers of Injustice," in Ephraim London, ed., *The Law as Literature* (New York: Simon and Schuster, 1960), p. 590.

CHAPTER 5

The Media Dilemma and Terrorism

Barry Rosen

FOR WEEKS during the summer of 1985, a daily crescendo of television news bulletins, specials, and newscasts brought the American people the drama of the hijacking of TWA Flight 847. Network morning news programs were full of the subject, and when there were no updates, they always had someone to interview. As is so often the case, the media became part of the story. Were the networks used by the terrorists? Were they undermining America's interests and weakening the government's ability to deal with the crisis? Did the network anchors cross the line separating journalism from diplomacy? To what extent did network competition affect the story?

These questions have been asked before—during the massacre of Israeli athletes at the 1972 Munich Olympics, the kidnapping of Patricia Hearst in 1974, the Hanafi Muslim takeover of three buildings in Washington in 1977, and, of course, during the captivity of the American hostages held in Iran from 1979 to 1981. Those questions will certainly be asked again when another incident occurs.

A replay of the debate over the proper place of television in the coverage of terrorism took place in the aftermath of the TWA incident. Prime Minister Thatcher urged news organizations to restrain their coverage of terrorism and remarked that television must "find ways to starve the terrorist . . . of the oxygen of publicity." United States Attorney General Edwin Meese endorsed the prime minister's comments and took her proposal a step further. He said that the U.S. government might ask news organizations to adopt a code of restraint and that broadcasters might be asked to agree to "some principles reduced to writing."

Any meeting between government and the Fourth Estate may provoke mixed emotions. The prospect of the government determining how television journalists should meet their responsibilities conjures up a vision of state control of information, perhaps leading to the British D-Notices. In Great Britain, the government formally notifies the press about security issues, and requests that information be withheld from the public. This is certainly not a system that I believe can work in the United States.

Subsequent to TWA Flight 847, a number of prominent news organizations, including UPI, the *Chicago Sun-Times*, and CBS News, independently drafted guidelines for the coverage of terrorist incidents and hostage-taking. These policies read something like "We should avoid providing an excessive platform for the terrorist," "there should be no live coverage of the terrorist," and "our coverage will not sensationalize a story beyond the fact of it being sensational." The guidelines attempt to shape responsible coverage and acknowledge that no specific, rules can exist for coverage of stories where facts and circumstances vary. To quote Dan Rather of CBS Evening News, "Journalism is not a precise science. . . . It is a crude art even on its best days."

Nevertheless, the inevitable relationship between TV and terrorists should not embarrass television news people or make them defensive. Terrorism is a product of modern life and as Russell Baker of the *New York Times* says, "It is not surprising that malcontents all over the world who believe they have just causes should spend their lives scheming to get a piece of the camera action."

The argument that television has become the terrorists' ultimate tool states that the granting of airtime to terrorists and to the events they stage-manage is akin to giving a credit card to assassins and bomb-throwers with which to shop the free world for sympathy and support. My wife, Barbara, who spent many hours appearing on television, articulates this view in an article she wrote for the *Wall Street Journal:*

> Have [U.S.] television journalists forgotten they are Americans? Everyone knows that terrorists want publicity for their cause, yet no less do they want to inflate their own personal status in their communities. . . . Therefore, each time the media afford the right to speak, they award them a victory!

I would, however, differ with my wife and the general argument. The drive to be first, combined with television's remarkable technology, is what makes for disturbing viewing. The most serious charge, therefore, is not really targeted toward television itself. A major reason that television was, for example, present in Beirut, is just that television exists; it has become a condition of being. Tom Wicker, the American columnist, made this point in 1985:

> It may on occasion be inconvenient, intrusive, even harmful; but if because of government censorship or network censorship the hostage crisis had not been visible, *real,* on American screens, the outrage and outcry would have been a thousand times louder than what's now being heard, and rightly so; for we depend on television for perception as we depend on air to breathe.

Much of the criticism of the media's hype of terrorism should be directed elsewhere. Although terrorists may in some respects dictate the script of an event that they have staged and determine in yet other ways the priorities of news coverage, the administration in Washington can also stage-manage much of the coverage. According to Hodding Carter III, the State Department spokesman during Jimmy Carter's presidency, "The government is not without resources to hold off or encourage a media presence." Six years after the Iran hostage crisis, he recalled that during a period of quiet negotiations with Latin American countries aimed at freeing us, he was ordered to stop talking about the hostages, and he said, "The story all but vanished." The Reagan administration, I suggest, raised the ante of the media coverage during the 847 incident, when it announced the president's vacation had been canceled and assigned presidential spokeman Larry Speakes the job of telling reporters—and through them, West Beirut's Shiites—that Reagan was considering the option of a blockade of Lebanon or of shutting down Beirut's airport. A signal was being sent.

What of the criticism that the media reports U.S. military movements and thus provides information that might be useful to hijackers and terrorists? Michael Burch, a Pentagon spokesman, has said, "For the price of a 19-inch television, a group of hijackers who only represent the back pew of some mosque have a very elaborate intelligence network." This issue was raised in 1985 in relation to media reports of the movement of the Delta Force from its U.S. base. From what I can gather in reading accounts of that incident, virtually all news organizations received information regarding military and diplomatic moves from government officials who provided it with the understanding that it was to be revealed. Network heads maintain that the reports were accurate and were promoted by the administration to send a message to the Shiites. Unless the United States was prepared to take direct military action in Beirut, the U.S. military presence was a symbol more than a threat, and symbols need to be appreciated.

Again, as the media reacts to charges of exploitation, the question is, Who is exploiting whom? Are the media furthering terrorist aims by providing extensive coverage? What's more, the public may be unduly alarmed and frightened, perhaps undermining its faith in the government as an institution that can ensure security and stability. In this case, the media face the possibility of becoming, in the public's view, unwitting allies of the terrorists. On the flip side, exclusively following the government line and interpretation opens the media to the charge of being the stooge and propaganda tool of the government. The media are damned if they do and damned if they don't.

Are the families truly exploited, or are the media, particularly television, helping to transmit information to families, to other Americans, and even to the U.S. government about how hostages are being treated? Are reporters keeping the issue alive for families who fear it will disappear in a diplomatic muddle? Indeed, many hostage families feel that the media, instead of invading their privacy, serve as a link to millions of sympathetic Americans and help make the crisis as important to others as it is to them. Peter Jennings, ABC's anchor, says that psychologists have told his staff that in some cases "there is actually a cathartic effect" for hostage families when they are in-

60   *Barry Rosen*

terviewed. He recalls that when the Marine compound was bombed in 1983, "people telephoned me and said, 'My son was killed, and why haven't you called me?' "

Nevertheless, a problem exists here. News executives, anchors, commentators, and correspondents skirt the issue. Many journalists and broadcasters embrace a philosophy that assumes a reality in the world that their job is to mirror accurately and recapture in all its detail so that an objective representation of the real world gets presented to their audience. The content of news broadcasts, however, at times suggests something else. This "reality" is filtered through an elaborate gatekeeping mechanism that screens and edits news content. Some news is, in effect, better than other news. Broadcast networks always keep an eye on ratings, on their competitors, and on the changing tastes of the audience. Crime news in the states has always done well, and terrorism, with its dramatic visual effects, is perfectly suited for television. That the media pursue their own self-interest and seek to sell the big story as effectively as they can is not surprising, even if, in some circumstances, this entails the gloss of melodramatics.

The dilemma the media face is real and pressing, with no palpable solutions at hand. If the media censor terrorist news, the decision may infringe on the public's right to know. In fact, the audience doesn't necessarily know what restraints journalism—television, radio, or print—may be imposing on itself. For instance, Lou Cannon of the *Washington Post* has pointed out that the press did not report that one hostage on Flight 847 was a member of the National Security Agency, which would have endangered him. On a local level, Lieutenant Robert T. Louden, the commanding officer of the New York City Police Department's Hostage Negotiating Team, echoes Cannon's remarks. Louden praises members of the media who respond to authorities' private pleas not to cover stories or aspects of stories that might result in harm to hostages or interfere with plans to take terrorists into custody.

Clearly, "objectivity" is, at best, difficult to approximate, much less to achieve. As the U.S. government has faltered in developing a policy for fighting terrorism that is grounded in both coherent and comprehensive principles yet still flexible enough to allow for effective response, so too has the media. Perhaps all that is possible to expect is that journalists make intelligent choices that require a sense of perspective. Perhaps less extensive and repetitive coverage that gives less airtime to terrorists is a beginning. Nevertheless, although the issues raised by terrorism are complex, they must not become a stalking-horse for depriving American citizens the access to a full account of events that affect their lives and their nation.

PART V

The UK Perspective

FOR MANY, democracy involves recognition of the inalienable right of the population to be informed about events. Without knowledge, citizens are unable to react properly or to assess a situation. The related right of free speech, enabling dissenters to express their views publicly, is equally valued. The role of the media within the United Kingdom or elsewhere is crucial to the maintenance of these freedoms. The existence of a varied media of high-quality and popular newspapers and broadcasting is seen as a healthy reflection of the level of freedoms enjoyed in Britain.

United Kingdom governmental control is effected formally through the Official Secrets Act, currently a subject of contention, and informally through the old-boy network and the lobby system. During crises, including those generated by terrorism, tensions between government and media come to the fore. The amount of information to be released to the press and the degree to which it should be disseminated by the media are crucial areas of contention. The coverage given to terrorists and their goals gives rise to conflict; in general, the media view is that terrorist views should be aired, provided that they are challenged.

Criticism of media coverage of terrorist leaders often involves the confusion of neutral reporting with actual support for their views. Despite overall acceptance that the public is able to grasp ideas, sift information, and decide issues for themselves, apparently they are assumed to be unable to do so when terrorism is involved. United Kingdom media people argue that the public is not naive about terrorism and is well able to deal with its propaganda in a rational and constructive way. They do not argue against all restrictions of information or against adjustment of its timing when immediate disclosure would endanger life and property. However, restriction in particular cases is not to be broadened to include general coverage. Official suspicion of media activity and a related movement toward increased censorship are reinforced by the traditional tendency of U.K. authorities to use a blanket of secrecy to cover everything from serious events to trivial facts about daily routine. Currently, the United Kingdom is having a lively debate on replacement of the Official Secrets Act by more selective legislation that would cover only serious issues of national security and on the introduction of a freedom-of-information act.

The comparative qualifications of U.K. officials and journalists to decide what is to be published are disputed. Given their access to better information, some of which may not be revealed, officials may feel better qualified. Journalists accept that they may make errors, but they take the view that, subject to some kind of restriction in crises, the public should receive the maximum possible information; the journalist should be judged competent to make his or her own decision as to what should be made public. Critics of this view point to the variable quality and ethics of journalists and are less sanguine about the public's capacity to judge an issue. They note that the media may misinform or mislead the public if balanced and clear reporting is not forthcoming. Confusion of terminology between "terrorist," "freedom fighter," "guerrilla," and the like is evident. A lack of balance is perceived in U.K. media reports; for example, Armenian terrorist attacks against Turkish diplomats are apparently justified through regular linkage with Turkish massacres of Armenians in the First World War, without presentation of a balancing Turkish point of view. Even if reporting is morally neutral, critics say it should actively support efforts to eradicate terrorist activity. Such views are countered, in turn, by the view that the evolution of British society has been possible only because dissent has been permitted; radical views should therefore be aired rather than suppressed, although their premises should be subject to constant questioning.

Further criticism concerns the training and qualifications required of journalists and the lack of accountability of journalists to the British public. The media reply that journalists primarily require a moral quality, a belief in discovering and publishing the truth, whereas accountability is perceived as residing with the individual journalist at the lowest level. Critics find such concepts to be too nebulous and doubt that the profession is effectively imbued with them. The introduction of censorship or licensing has been proposed to raise media ethics and performance, but such proposals are rejected by much of the media as representing too great an infringement on their capacity to operate effectively. A general aura of mutual suspicion governs overall government-press relations, and it is reflected in their interaction regarding terrorism.

This situation has given rise to disenchantment with the U.K. press in some quarters. Censorship of the British press was introduced during the two world wars and was accepted in the national interest. Media abuse of its privileges regarding terrorism is such that censorship may again be considered. Media reporting in Northern Ireland has been much criticized for its desire to secure exclusive reports (scoops), often under cover of the public's right to know. Some argue that media involvement inevitably serves to complicate the task of the security forces and that the media should adopt a low profile. Doubt exists as to the media's capacity to fulfill such a role, and various proposals, including self-discipline within the profession, action through the courts, and direct government action, have been considered in the British context to inculcate the sense of responsibility that some believe is lacking. Voluntary restraint in newspapers is viewed as requiring a radical change of attitude by their owners because the behavior of journalists regarding terrorism is strongly affected by the views of their employers. However, given a belief that such a change is unlikely, recourse to the courts, which act slowly, or to government action is deemed likely.

The revision of the Official Secrets Act provides a crucial focus for U.K. government-media differences. Advocates of reform note that the act requires revision because it is inappropriate for modern requirements; it was passed in 1911 and remains largely unamended. Section 2 is held to be in such disrepute that juries reject cases based on its provisions, resulting in government use of legal injunctions to control dissemination of information. A revised act dealing only with international relations, terrorism, the Foreign and Commonwealth Office, and certain financial matters has been proposed. However, a revision would probably introduce stronger sanctions against publication of information in these areas; the net effect would thus be to reduce public access.

CHAPTER 6

Terrorism, Journalism, and Democracy

Alan H. Protheroe, MBE, TD, FBIM

JOURNALISM is about discovery and disclosure. That is its raison d'être; that is the rationale supporting it. In a society with a controlled media, the task of government is, in the short term, made very easy: apply the necessary sanctions and either extinguish the media that do not support and agree with the government or make sure that the only communications systems in the country are owned, operated, and controlled by the government. That way, a government will have a docile public, a public knowing only what authority believes is good for them to know. In these circumstances, the government can—in theory anyway—do what it likes, when it likes, how it likes, and where it likes. But it doesn't work.

To my mind, the press and publishing restrictions currently being applied in South Africa exemplify the paradox that arises. South Africa proclaims itself to be a Westernized, high-tech nation embracing the traditional democratic values. Although the South African idea of democracy may perfectly properly be quibbled about when large numbers of the population are disenfranchised, hitherto the government's attitude toward the media has not been an object of criticism. For years, South Africa had the freest and most unfettered press on that continent. Then, suddenly, new sets of restrictions were imposed that virtually prevent any kind of reporting of the social and political turmoil there. In one morning, South Africa had put itself firmly behind an iron curtain of information controls. The excuse is that the threat of terrorism is too great and that publicity will encourage the African National Congress (ANC) to greater excesses. "South Africa," said one government minister to me, "is at war. Even in Europe, you don't hesitate to censor and control the media in such a crisis."

This argument is not without its superficial—but somewhat simplistic—attractions. It begs many questions, however, not least the right of the citizen to know what is being done—or not done—in his or her name. Does it also raise an even more fundamental question? Terrorism can be a last-resort argument. Perhaps the democratic state itself attracts problems if it

64

fails to give the dissenting voice the opportunity for a hearing, usually obtained through a free press.

A democracy must have free, unfettered, undirected, but responsible media. Without that, people are deprived of that spectrum of data on which to make up their minds. The task of journalism is not to tell people what to think; it is to provide information for people to use in their thinking. Once directed, controlled media are in place, a credibility chasm develops between electorate and government that strikes at the heart of what all of us in the United Kingdom stand for. Be quite clear that, despite "controls," people hear of events and incidents that, they quickly notice, are not being reported in their own media. In short order, the government is placed at risk, the more so when citizens realize that elsewhere in the world free media report the undisclosed machinations of the state in which they live.

In a democracy, things are both different and more difficult. A democracy has a multiplicity of voices, opinions, and attitudes; some are angry, others awkward, and a few potentially dangerous. The degree to which a democracy permits the audibility of those more difficult voices poses one of the problems that add up to what I choose to call "the democratic dilemma."

In a democracy, I believe that the dissident and even the dangerous voices must be heard, not least because nothing angers me more than the arrogant assumption by those in power that the public is not capable of differentiating between good and evil and that the public needs to be led. The public is more than capable of making up its own mind, without directed thought from officialdom. The public—in Britain, anyway—has consistently demonstrated its capacity to understand some complex and abstract concepts—territorial integrity, for example—and to recognize truth. However, it learns to differentiate, I submit, through the efforts of free, unfettered, responsible media.

I perceive a recurring conflict between journalists on the one hand and, on the other, those who wish to manipulate society. Let us leave out of the equation those who try to have a foot in both camps, for some journalists as well as some politicians see broadcasting and newspapers as instruments to achieve an end, and both are indulging in their own manipulative attempts.

The vast majority of journalists are, in fact, people of integrity—straightforward, hardworking, talented men and women whose task is to discover—knowing they have no God-given right to an answer to their questions—and to disclose fairly, accurately, and dispassionately. The point of collision is there, of course. Disclosure generates the attacks from those who feel that unless every syllable written or spoken supports their own view of the world, then journalists are contributing to disorder and upsetting the status quo.

That people prefer not to hear bad news is nothing new, certainly, and politicians are particularly averse to hearing it. Now, however, I detect a

growing wish not to know much about what is going on. This trend may be
part of our collective guilt about the problems we face in this country and
elsewhere in the world, yet the nation divides itself a little more each day.
Tensions exist that are in no way eased by the political investment by all
sides. In this climate, the journalist simply has to accept that doing the job
in any meaningful way inevitably leads to knee-jerk criticism and reactive
hysteria that will hit the journalist with all the force of a heavyweight wres-
tler's kick in the groin.

The ultimate test I apply in the decision to publish a story is straightforward: does the publication of that particular piece of information increase
the sum of knowledge available to the public so that they may better understand what is happening around them? That criterion is not as easy as it
sounds, for the journalist must also be aware that large numbers of people
want to be sheltered from the truth and from unpalatable facts; they seek
only the constant reinforcement of their prejudices, and woe betide the journalist who dares to report something that runs counter to those preconceptions. If, as required, we journalists present the arguments for and against
any single proposition, and if we report the opposing view, whether about
intended legislation or new concepts in industry, medicine, science, or the
arts, then many people feel the boat is being rocked and traditions are being
challenged. Those who felt secure in their beliefs might regard any challenge
as a "threat to be extinguished," a "threat to democracy itself." This self-
induced intellectual anesthesia, this unwillingness to even imagine the possibility that someone who does not hold your particular view could be right,
the rejection of argument, the refusal to contemplate alternatives, and the
determination not even to consider why something might require adjustment
do exist and are identifiable.

Reporting terrorism is necessary. Let us make a clear distinction between reporting the consequences (and the background) of terrorism and the
advocacy of terrorism. No one, anywhere, must provide an open platform
or an unchallenged opportunity for the advocacy of terrorism. Nevertheless,
the problem facing a democratic society remains; for the maintenance of
democracy, unpopular, even dangerous views must be heard and thoroughly
understood. I will not accept that the British public is so foolish or so naive
as to accept the rationality of the arguments put forward by the proponents
of terrorism, however charismatic they may seem, however sincerely they
appear to hold their dreadful beliefs, and however well articulated their philosophies.

Northern Ireland is a recurring challenge to us in this matter of reporting
terrorism. It also exemplifies this "democratic dilemma." Legitimizing Sinn
Fein was a bold and courageous decision, designed to divert republicanism
from the Armalite toward the ballot box. It could not possibly succeed, for
all Sinn Fein supporters are axiomatically committed to the maintenance of
what they call "the armed struggle." So the democratic electoral process
serves to domesticate the supporters of terrorism. In those terms, those who
support it must advocate it.

The dilemma, then, for a democratically elected government is this: should the expression of views by the supporters of terrorism be silenced, even when those views are implicit in the political backgrounds of democratically elected individuals at local council, assembly, or parliament level? Can government say, in effect, "You can report Sinn Fein supporters if they're talking about the drains in Londonderry or the state of the pavements in West Belfast, but you can't report them if they mutter a word about the need for the 'maintenance of the armed struggle' "? If government wants to say that, then it should say it. Let government proscribe and let it legislate, but even government can't have it both ways.

Certainly, the experience in Northern Ireland has demonstrated one thing very clearly: the consequences of terrorism must be reported. This view is shared by, for example, the Royal Ulster Constabulary and the armed forces. Accurate and swift reportage prevents the spread of rumor and the further escalation of violence. Down through the years, the responsible media have diligently and accurately reported Northern Ireland affairs. We have fully reported the violence there—we could hardly avoid that—and the tensions as well. One of the ways in which we have tried to assist a proper understanding of the facts has very occasionally been to talk to members of certain organizations. An enormous, politically generated public fuss ensues each time on the very rare occasions we broadcast one of these interviews. The BBC has a detailed procedure for its journalists to go through before such an interview can be recorded—let alone broadcast—and permission is given only when the journalist demonstrates that the interview will provide information that will allow people to make up their own minds.

Reporting about and quoting terrorists is not new. Newspapers do it all the time. Radio and television do have a greater impact, but if we are never to report these attitudes, how then would we get behind the headlines of killings and bombings? How can we inform, explain, and enlighten? One constant criticism of the headline style of reporting is that it fosters a bland acceptance of the situation. I have no hesitation in defending the right to err on the side of free speech, in the interest of greater understanding, on this and other matters.

When BBC Television broadcast an interview with a member of the Irish National Liberation Army some months after they had killed a senior politician (Airey Neave), audience research showed that 80 percent of the public approved the decision to broadcast, and an overwhelming majority found themselves even more antagonistic to the aims and actions of the terrorist groups at the end of the program than they had been before. If we, as individuals, subscribe to the concept of democracy, then we must, axiomatically, subscribe to the ideal of freedom of information, for that is the source of knowledge from which understanding develops. Intelligent judgments can be based only on understanding and knowledge.

Many people would like to believe that ignoring something makes it quietly go away. It doesn't. Not reporting a bomb, for example, would not prevent other bombs; indeed, I suspect that the next would be even bigger.

Then the corollary problem develops that people would begin to wonder what else was not being reported. In fairly short order, confidence in government and the forces of law and order would erode. Let me repeat: reporting the effects of terrorism and questioning the philosophy of terrorism are entirely different from the advocacy of terrorism.

Another glib argument, of course, is the repetition of those old saws about "the only bad publicity is no publicity" and "it doesn't matter what they say as long as they spell your name right." I have heard them all by now, and none of the slick sayings stands up under close examination. Alongside the spouting of such trivia is the belief—and I am always astonished by the number of apparently intelligent people who fall into this trap—that reporting terrorism is synonymous with approving of it. What nonsense! Who can approve of mindless violence and the destruction of lives? For those of us who have witnessed and experienced terrorism at first hand, who have taken up arms against terrorism, and who have experienced the comforting presence of plainclothes personal-protection officers, the reality of terrorism is a stark reality indeed.

To a certain extent, the terrorist captures the media. The best interests of the terrorists lie in representing themselves as Robin Hoods forced by an unsympathetic—indeed hostile!—world to resort to acts of violence, destruction, and death in their efforts to right the terrible injustices suffered by their race, ethnic group, or coreligionists. Few can sustain such a facade, for the media too are not as gullible as many would wish to believe. Terrorist leaders frequently wish to portray themselves as romantics or as thwarted statesmen, again driven (they would say against their will) to take up arms against society and to outlaw themselves in the great cause; terrorism, they seem to suggest, is their court of last resort.

The conspiratorial nature that surrounds a meeting between a terrorist leader and a journalist is in itself fascinating. I had such an experience some years ago when I arranged to meet a leading terrorist in Beirut. I was told to wait for the call in the foyer of the Commodore Hotel. At three o'clock in the morning, a suave messenger told me to come with him. We had a high-speed journey in the small convoy of cars, round and about the darkened streets, and entered an apartment block seething with heavily armed men—the kind of scene to quicken the blood of any journalist—until I reminded myself of what the organization stood for. Yes, it was a publicity stunt. I saw through it, as it happens. Others, less experienced, might have been captured by it all. In that area, a particular problem emerges. Part of the difficulty for the media is to determine when a terrorist stunt is just that, a stunt designed for the media. From whom do we take advice? Who is really qualified to advise us that it is just a publicity stunt? Is one letter bomb that actually explodes and for which responsibility is claimed by a hitherto unknown group merely a stunt, or is it evidence that a new group really is at work? Do we wait for the second bomb, when publicity for the first might have alerted people to be on the lookout? The responsibility is horrendous, and the judgments cannot be the media's alone.

Censorship, proscription, control of the media, short-circuit procedures for the extradition of persons accused on terrorist offenses, snatch squads to lift known terrorists from their havens, military raids on countries known to support and finance terrorism—all these have been and are being considered and tried these days. A convincing and coherent emotional argument can be adduced to support these actions; be perfectly clear that I have no answers at all. Still, those measures are definable as being antidemocratic in the real sense of the concept. Where, in all that, stands another cornerstone of democracy, the rule of law?

In the final analysis, journalism, like every other aspect of society, has to examine itself in the context of what I perceive to be a philosophical, judicial, moral, and political dilemma: how far may a democratic society go in adopting and implementing fundamentally antidemocratic measures ostensibly designed to protect that democratic society without damaging and rapidly extinguishing the concept of democracy on which that society is predicated? This dilemma is the basis for a rich and worthwhile debate, a debate I have been seeking to generate—with little success, I must confess—but one I deeply and passionately believe needs to take place. It is a debate that must emerge in the context of this changing, turbulent, political, censorious, frightening, and wonderful world of ours. It is a debate in which all must join; it is a debate to which all must contribute.

PART VI

The European
Perspective

T HE EVIDENT CONTROVERSY in the United Kingdom over
the media's role in terrorism is inevitably mirrored to some
degree in all countries. However, certain West European
countries have evolved ground rules to limit conflict and to
introduce a basis for government-media cooperation. The case of
Denmark provides an example of this process.

In recent years, the Danish government has established a cooperative relationship with the country's radio and television broadcasters
regarding terrorism. It was partially modeled on earlier arrangements
for handling natural disasters. Essential features of the arrangement
include regular provision of government information to the media,
keeping the public informed, arrangements to ensure that the counterterrorist is not hindered, and maintenance of media independence. The system is in place and has operated successfully on a
number of occasions.

However, tensions inevitably arise because the media and authorities have different functions in a crisis: the media are concerned with
informing people, the right to know, and their own independence;
officials have different concerns and resent an intrusive media presence. This division is the principal obstacle to cooperation. Both parties may recognize this tension and seek alternatives enabling positive
relations do develop. Government action has four possible courses.

1. The authorities assume full control of the dissemination of information and news through the media.

2. The authorities take partial control through authoritative statements issued by broadcasting editors, speaker services, and presentation departments, while the dissemination of news continues simultaneously along normal lines and uncoordinated with the authorities' statements.

3. The authorities release a limited number of communiqués for normal newscasts but otherwise handle the direct communication of information to the public along their own channels and using siren alerts, loudspeaker vans, personal contact to involved groups, and other direct means.

4. Cooperation is established between the authorities and one or a few electronic public mass media, where the communication of information and news is coordinated.

Full control by the authorities is generally felt to be unacceptable within a democracy. Also, the initial advantage accruing to the authorities dissipates as the population learns that news is not coming from the usual independent sources. The use of official spokespersons alongside regular news staff enables information to be presented as the government wishes, but an unskilled spokesperson may not be convincing, and contradictions may arise between government and regular news staff that cause credibility problems. Similar problems may arise with the third option. A cooperative media-government relationship enables coordination on information released and clear identification of its source. The independence of both is compromised to some degree. However, within a cooperative environment, differences are more easily resolved. The few terrorist situations arising in the country have been dealt with through open cooperation, enabling both parties to influence decisions on the release of information and other matters. The media may feel unable to black out an item entirely, but they respect requests that help to save lives.

For such a system to work in Denmark—and probably elsewhere—regular discussions between the two sides are necessary, and clear, agreed-upon results have to be produced. Officials dealing with terrorism and the media people concerned need to be well acquainted to generate the essential mutual confidence. The role of the media remains independent, and decisions are taken by management at the most senior level.

The application of such a system in other countries may encounter problems, particularly if the electronic media are fragmented. All four options involve some restrictions on reporting, and these may be possible only under state-of-emergency provisions that governments may not wish to invoke because they enhance the credibility of terrorists; however, informal arrangements may offer an alternative. Overall, the Danish systems may be said to involve self-restraint rather than self-censorship. Application of this philosophy may represent a compromise to solve the dilemmas described earlier.

CHAPTER 7

The Scope and Limits of Cooperation Between the Media and the Authorities

Søren Elmquist

IN A TERRORIST SITUATION, conflicts inevitably occur between the authorities and the media, and the question is whether that could be improved in a way that the fundamental obligations for both parts are respected. Could and should the media cooperate actively with the authorities in such a situation?

The first time I myself had to face this question in practice was seven years ago when I was still chief subeditor of the radio news department of the Danish Broadcasting Corporation. A plane from Athens was hijacked, and the hijackers commanded it to go to Copenhagen. The information was received from the international news bureaus at an early stage so that we had plenty of time to make preparations to cover the arrival at Copenhagen Airport and what was to come afterward.

One previous situation had involved a hijacked plane in Denmark, but that was a short episode that ended quite undramatically with the hijacker's surrender when the plane was still in the air, so Denmark had no real experience in covering such a situation where a terrorist action went on for a long period on Danish soil. We had to consider how to try to establish some kind of coordination or cooperation with the authorities.

The background for these reflections is that the Danish Broadcasting Corporation (DBC) is the official, public, national Danish radio and television company; it is owned by the state but is completely independent. However, the DBC has a special responsibility to the population and to Danish society as a whole to report what is going on and to ensure that information is as close to reality as is possible. I thought it would be foolish and irrational not to try to establish some fixed contact channels with the authorities to secure effective and substantial research on likely news angles, to be able to check with the competent authorities that the information broadcast was true and precise, to organize a system that enabled us to get in touch promptly with relevant individuals from the authorities for interviews and comments, and to enable the authorities to get messages to the public via radio; all relate to the population's right to know. Media independence was to be retained, as was the right to remain critical and to make independent decisions on editorial matters on behalf of the population. However, establishing an effective net of contact channels to secure communication and thereby reduce the risks of conflicts between the authorities and official Danish radio was in the interest of everybody involved.

A similar setup for coordination of crisis management already existed between the authorities and the Danish Broadcasting Corporation but only in a specific and strictly civil area, such as the risk of disaster caused by floods in some parts of Denmark. However, I was inspired by that agreement when I got the idea of establishing contacts with the authorities in the hijack situation.

Initial contact was made with the special staff in the foreign office dealing with such matters to propose establishing a setup, which was rejected. The reaction was very negative. A subsequent direct contact with the foreign secretary produced a positive reaction; he realized the advantages in the proposition for the authorities, for the broadcasters, and for the population.

Shortly afterward, the hijackers changed the destination of the plane, and it landed in London a few hours later. Yet this episode led to constructive discussions that later resulted in an official agreement to cooperate in making specific arrangements for informing the population about large-scale disasters and crises—civil as well as military. The agreement has been put to use and the cooperation system based on it has been used and cultivated since then, both in practice and in exercises. Also, coverage of later terrorism has been based on this agreement.

Entering into real cooperation in the true sense of the word presents fundamental problems. The largest problem derives from the fact that the media and the authorities have different functions in society in terrorist situations; authorities have to act quickly and improvise, and the population has to be informed. The authorities' functions are to analyze the situation, lay out a strategy for tackling the problem, make decisions, and try to get the people involved or the population to react in specific ways. The media have two functions: to inform the population, in clear respect of the right to know; and to cover journalistically what is going on, including acting as the Fourth Estate and being the citizens' representative.

That difference almost automatically creates a schism or even a conflict between the authorities and the media people. The two cannot simply work together in handling the situation because the authorities do not wish to be controlled by the media, and the media must, along with informing the population, watch the authorities carefully and critically, as this is also their task. Thus, built into the relationship is an antagonism that often leads directly to mistrust. Many public servants—civil as well as military—feel that journalists are spying on them and consequently dare not rely on them, and many journalists are convinced that even the slightest cooperation with the authorities is a threat to their journalistic integrity. This schism or conflict is the strongest obstacle to cooperation and coordination. The authorities and media have different functions and different obligations that sometimes inevitably end in conflicts over principles. Consequently, total and definite cooperation is impossible, and that has been the conclusion of the negotiations in Denmark between the authorities and the media. We have to face the fact that the necessary mutual respect of each other's right to make decisions and fulfill our respective fundamental obligations is incompatible with joining forces in complete cooperation.

The question then is if other ways can better the relationship between the authorities and the media so that attitudes are not hostile and conflictual but professional and characterized by mutual respect for each other's functions and obligations.

To find the answer to this question, we can look at how the relationship between the authorities and the electronic mass media actually is handled when there are large-scale disasters and crises, civil as well as military, around the world. Again I do not concentrate on terrorist situations in the narrow meaning of the term but choose to include them as a subgroup of the larger category of crisis situations. Experiences from crisis management generally can be appropriately used.

I examine the electronic mass media and not other outlets such as newspapers and news magazines. The main reason has been stated by a respected, professional editor in chief of a newspaper. In a discussion about coverage of terrorist situations, he said that all essential ethical decisions are made in practice by the electronic mass media simply because they are on air from second to second and the newspapers simply have to follow their decisions. If they do not, their actions will solely be a matter of historical interest hours after the event—a drastic way to put it but quite close to reality.

The relationship between the authorities and the electronic mass media generally develops according to one of the following four principal models:

1. The authorities assume full control of the dissemination of information and news through the media.

2. The authorities take control to some extent, often through authoritative statements issued by broadcasting editors, speaker services, and presentation departments, while dissemination of news continues simultaneously along normal lines and is uncoordinated with the authoritative statements.

3. The authorities release a limited number of authoritative communiqués for normal newscasts but otherwise handle the direct communication of information to the public along their own channels using siren alerts, loudspeaker vans, personal contact to specially involved groups, and other methods.

4. The fourth model is characterized by the fact that cooperation is established between the authorities and one or a few electronic public mass

media, where the communication of information and news is coordinated.

Each of the four models involve a number of advantages and disadvantages. In the first model, in which the authorities take full control of the dissemination of official information as well as the news coverage, control can be gained by the direct method of sending representatives of the authorities directly to the microphones. More often, however, and in a more indirect manner, authorities dictate what is to be passed on to the population and demand the right to approve news information before it is broadcast. Another word for it is "censorship."

Apart from the fact that this model, in my opinion, is totally unacceptable in relation to democratic principles including the freedom of the press, it certainly has a clear advantage from the authorities' point of view in that the handling of information may be fully adjusted to the overall emergency strategy. However, their credibility will suffer seriously as the population realizes that the information does not originate from the normal sources and is not being handled in the usual way. Accordingly, they risk "underground" news dissemination resulting in the spreading of rumors and public disturbances.

In the second model, authorities take control to some extent by dictating official alert messages via the electronic mass media to be presented by the official speaker service. In this case, the normal news staff must not be dealing with the problem. On the contrary, the news staff is performing normal news coverage of the situation totally independent of the official alert messages presented on the same channel. This model also has a number of advantages and disadvantages. Official spokespersons tend not to be competent and capable of handling the function. Their normal job does not give them sufficient practice to handle such dramatic and demanding problems in which the time pressures and demands of correctness are high. News journalists are the ones who are used to dealing with such problems. However, this model ensures that the information that, according to the judgment of the authorities, is necessary and relevant does in fact reach the public in exactly the form they deem appropriate. However, they are unable to control or even have any real influence on the parallel, normal handling of news, with the result that contradictory information and duplicate messages are inevitably communicated to the population. Again, credibility problems and public disturbances naturally result.

The third model involves the authorities trying to handle the information as much as possible by themselves by means of siren alerts, loudspeaker vans, emergency information material, and personal contact to specially involved groups, while the mass media are provided with only a limited number of authoritative communiqués for normal newscasts. This model is typically used in regional disaster situations, but it has also been practiced on a large scale. It is applicable for many terrorist situations where the authorities try to erect smoke screens. This model offers the advantage that the authorities may put their entire effort into internal measures, including goal-directed handling of information, but the effect will be highly incomplete and the authorities' influence on the mass media practically nonexistent. The media can alter the official communiqués without any kind of consultation with the authorities, and changes can result in mistakes not necessarily because of manipulation but because special, direct connections between the authorities and the mass media do not exist.

The last model, the coordination, or cooperation, model, involves coordination between the authorities and one or a few electronic mass media in order to inform the population. It involves both official information and news information, and therefore the news departments are dealing with it as a connected whole. This model ensures a steady, continuous coordination of all information to the population via both the authoritative statements and the news broadcasts. For both categories, they are broadcast by the news editors with a distinct indication of source as far as the authoritative statements are concerned.

The disadvantage of this model is that both official authority in relation to information matters and the integrity of the press are put to a serious test. Nonetheless, this model has been given priority in Denmark in recent years. The medium chosen there is the radio because of the simple fact that, when a national crisis situation, civil or military, develops into something really serious, the electricity may fail and almost all TV sets will be inoperative, whereas everybody has battery-powered radios. The underlying principle for the cooperation model is that the authorities together with a responsible, public mass medium must have the common, ideal, overall goal in an emergency situation of ensuring that the population is made aware of and is given the opportunity to understand the conditions that are decisive for the individual citizen in the given situation, knowledge and understanding that are essential for each individual to react in the most rational manner possible. This is the best way to proceed, at least in the democratic societies of the Western world.

Inevitably, of course, controversies and conflicts of interest occur between the authorities and the news departments, but let me give you an example that shows that in practice such problems often diminish. In a crisis situation, the authorities have the right to present an official alert message to the designated electronic mass medium or media. If it is clear, understandable, and without problems, it is broadcast by the news staff at once, with a distinct indication of source. If it involves problems, the news editors at once point them out to the authorities, rapid analyses and discussions will take place, and a conclusion should be reached within a short time.

In Denmark this system is, as I have said, founded on an agreement between the authorities and the Danish Broadcasting Corporation. In this agreement the radio system has agreed to broadcast official alert messages from the authorities on demand and if some specific criteria are fulfilled. These criteria are that the message must present information with the purpose of relieving an acute, life-threatening situation. In principle, therefore, the authorities can force the radio service to broadcast such messages if the criteria in their opinion are fulfilled, no matter what. However, in reality and in practice this situation has never occurred and will probably never occur because of two circumstances. First, the authorities have been and are so reasonable that they realize that the pointing out of problems in communication indicates that they may have problems they are not aware of; second, everybody realizes that the first definite demand that is presented may very well mark the end of successful cooperation.

Along with the official alert messages from the authorities, these situations are covered according to normal journalistic procedures, meaning that interviews with and statements from experts from the authorities are provided as well as with independent or alternative commentators. Reporters are not bound or obliged to present these interviews and statements to the authorities, but often they do, of course, in order to have the authorities' reactions and comments on them. Here the cooperation system that enables contact with the authorities without veto power over broadcasting an interview or a statement is enormously useful. The media attitude is and must be that it cannot hold back relevant and serious information because doing so would ruin our reliability, a dangerous matter not only for the media but for the whole society and perhaps especially in tense situations like those we are dealing with here.

Exceptions exist, of course, when lives are at stake, in war situations, or in terrorist situations, for instance, or when we might unintentionally inform an enemy or terrorists who are listening to the radio. Despite the exceptions, the principle must be that essential information is not withheld and that the media decides; otherwise, nobody would trust the media in peacetime or in wartime, and that situation would be a threat to democracy as a whole.

The Danish cooperation model has proven its possibilities in a number of situations: where risk of explosions in or spillage from factories has made the authorities implement emergency measures, in connection with the Chernobyl accident, and in connection with a great number of exercises, such as military crisis-management exercises and hijacking exercises.

Not many terrorist situations have developed in Denmark. In some episodes with bomb attacks and terror killings and a few embassy occupations in the last couple of years, we have operated on the basis of the cooperation model to the satisfaction of both the radio station and the authorities. What is essential is the creation of a climate and a communication system between the radio news department and the authorities, the police, the military forces, the different civil authorities, and so on that in crisis situations makes possible and natural the exchange of points of view, arguments over the information content, and analysis. In other words, an attitude of openness and mutual respect can be established via this setup so that each can accept the other's decisions and include the other's arguments in decision-making.

I would probably never find myself in a situation in which I could be convinced by the authorities to remain totally silent about a terrorist action going on because of the risk of making propaganda for terrorism. I do not believe in manipulating reality like that, but I could be faced with arguments so strong that I accepted keeping the coverage to a minimum. In the same way, I could not be talked into broadcasting false or fake information, but I could be persuaded not to broadcast information about an action to free hostages if the arguments presented convinced me that lives were at stake.

In Denmark this setup works in the relationship between the authorities and the radio news department of the Danish Broadcasting Corporation. It has also gradually developed with the TV news department, and we intend to bring it into practice in future crisis situations of all kinds. During the last few years, I have several times presented it to representatives of other countries' media and authorities and have noticed very positive reactions, especially from the other Nordic countries, Canada, the Netherlands, West Germany, the United States, and the United Kingdom.

Obviously, however, a cooperative setup like this is not something to be invented and made operative from one day to another. Time has to be spent analyzing and developing it and establishing a number of prerequisites.

- A thorough round of discussions between competent people from the authorities and competent people from the media must take place in which the relevant problems are pointed out and analyzed and the different functions and roles defined.

- A clear, simple, unambiguous fixing of the decision-making process must be developed, concentrating on a few people on each side, including direct access to those with top decision-making authority.

- The people involved from both sides must be instructed in the plans and the whole setup, preferably together, to achieve mutual personal knowledge, and frequent exercises with the participation of both parties are essential.

- Perhaps most important, mutual confidence and trust must be established so that the collaborative partners, whether they are civil servants or journalists, heads or staff, will act rationally and in conformity with the spirit of the whole setup. This relationship prevents the time-consuming and exasperating reexamination of other people's actions that in a short time would prove to be fatal to the underlying, leading principle: cooperation.

PART VII

Appendices

APPENDIX A

Selected Papers

Editors' Note: The following appendix includes three papers representing some aspects of the topic of terrorism and the media that were not covered in detail at the Wilton Park Security Conference. These papers were commissioned by the Terrorism and the News Media Research Project, directed by Professor Robert G. Picard of Emerson College in Boston, and are reprinted by permission.

1 | Network Evening News Coverage of the TWA Hostage Crisis

Tony Atwater, Ph.D., Michigan State University

A series of international terrorist activities during the 1980s has focused attention on the role of the media in publicizing such incidents. In 1985 and 1986 the television networks devoted extensive news coverage to the TWA hostage crisis, the *Achille Lauro* hijacking, the Malta debacle, and the Rome/Vienna airport bombings. By providing extensive and continuous coverage of terrorist events, television networks risk giving a platform to terrorist grievances. Laqueur has asserted that the success of a terrorist operation depends heavily on the amount of publicity it receives.[1]

The potential for becoming participants in terrorist acts requires additional discretion on the part of television journalists. In the political arena, media coverage of terrorist activities has sometimes been interpreted as an element of pressure on government to promptly resolve what citizens may regard as a national crisis. Alexander has observed that through excessive news coverage "establishment" communications channels willingly or unwillingly become tools in the terrorist strategy.[2]

Adams has noted that the accusation that excessive media coverage legitimizes terrorist interests warrants documentation before we can accept such a charge as factual.[3] The purpose of this study was to investigate the amount and nature of news coverage devoted to the hijacking of Trans World Airlines Flight 847 on June 14, 1985. Studies on media coverage of hostage crises help journalists and consumers to become more knowledgeable about conventions in news coverage of international terrorism.

The daily network news broadcast provides a major outlet upon which many Americans rely for news of the day. Further, the agenda-setting potential of television warrants-that social scientists explore audience implications of detailed coverage of terrorism.[4] An individual network's daily news coverage of a hostage crisis may send a message to viewers by the emphasis the evening news gives the event. This study analyzed the extent of coverage the networks devoted to a terrorist event in their evening news broadcasts. The study is unique in its analysis of the complete time period of the crisis from the seizure of the American hostages aboard TWA Flight 847 (June 14, 1985) until their release (June 30, 1985). The study adds to earlier analyses of network news coverage of crises that have attempted to convey insight into the nature, rationale, and emphasis of network news content on terrorism.

RELATED STUDIES

Several previous studies have examined network evening news coverage of the Iranian hostage crisis of 1979. Altheide found no significant differences among the networks in the number of reports and topics covered relative to the crisis.[5] He noted that reports on the instability and volatility of the Iranian government characterized the evening news broadcasts of all three networks. In another study of the Iranian hostage crisis, Meeske and Javaheri again found similarity among the networks in that they were neutral in terms of expressing bias for or against the U.S. and Iran.[6]

In a later study, Altheide found that certain topics received varied amounts of network coverage during the Iranian hostage crisis.[7] He observed that the reporting of selected events corresponded with criteria of production formats such as visual quality, thematic unity, and accessibility. Similarity in organization and format among networks contributed to consonance or homogeneity in network reports of the hostage crisis.

Although much has been written about the similarity of how the networks covered the Iranian hostage crisis, Nimmo and Combs reported that the three networks exhibited differing thematic emphases and foci of coverage.[8] The authors also noted that the networks differed in the persons selected as news sources. NBC, for example, was found to have relied more heavily on average citizens in the network's reports on the crisis.

Paletz, Ayanian, and Fozzard studied network coverage of three terrorist groups and found that the networks reported the same events and portrayed them similarly.[9] The researchers concluded that television news did not endow terrorists with legitimacy and that the justness of terrorist causes was denied. A fault of network coverage, according to the authors, was its failure to adequately reflect upon the underlying objectives behind terrorist acts.

RESEARCH QUESTIONS

The period examined was June 14 to June 30, 1985, which encompassed the day on which the hostages were seized to the time of their eventual release. The extent of coverage devoted to reports on the hostage crisis was the central issue to be investigated. Several specific research questions that the study addressed included the following:

1. What was the amount of coverage devoted to the crisis daily in each network's evening news broadcast?
2. What types of stories did hostage reports frequently involve (anchor, reporter, commentary)?
3. What topics did the evening news broadcasts emphasize in covering the TWA hostage crisis?
4. What percentage of news time did network evening newscasts devote to the crisis daily?
5. Where did most reports on the TWA hostage crisis originate?

METHOD

A comprehensive content analysis of TWA hostage reports broadcast on "ABC World News Tonight," "CBS Evening News," and "NBC Nightly News" was undertaken to address the above issues. Comprehensive, compiled videotapes of these reports were obtained from the Vanderbilt University Television News Archive. All TWA hostage stories broadcast by the evening news programs between June 14 and June 30, 1985, were included in the analysis. Each story was coded with the aid of a two-page protocol for story type, story topic, origin of report, length of story, and network identification.

The unit of analysis was the news story, which was defined as "any topic introduced by the anchor person coupled with any report or reports by other correspondents on the same topic and any concluding remarks by the anchor person."[10] Each news item was coded according to type as either an anchor story, reporter story, or commentary/analysis. This typology was used to specify the main presenter of the story and to distinguish news items from commentaries.[11]

STORY TOPIC

Each TWA hostage story was coded into one of seventeen topic categories that corresponded to the topic principally featured in the report. Several of the topic categories were developed after a preliminary review of videotapes and news transcripts. The other topic categories used in the analysis were based on Altheide's study of the Iranian hostage crisis.[12]

STORY ORIGIN

To ascertain the proximity from which stories were filed on the crisis, four categories were used to describe story origin. Those categories included: (1) Washington/New York; (2) USA/Other; (3) Beirut/Lebanon; and (4) London/Other. Because all three network newscasts typically originate from New York, anchor-read stories were coded Washington/New York, unless reported from another location. An additional category, "Location Not Given," was used when a report, other than an anchor-read story, failed to indicate place of origin. The category USA/Other was assigned to stories from U.S. cities other than Washington, D.C., or New York. The category London/Other was assigned to those stories filed from London and other cities and countries other than London, England, and Beirut, Lebanon.

NEWS TIME

Each hostage story broadcast on the three evening newscasts was coded in seconds with the aid of a stopwatch. In addition, a measure of the "news hole" for each of the fifty-one newscasts was computed by eliminating time

Appendix A

Table 1. Number of Network Hostage Reports by Day

Newscast Day	ABC	CBS	NBC	Total
June 14	6	6	9	21
June 15	11	13	6	30
June 16	14	13	13	40
June 17	13	11	10	34
June 18	17	10	12	39
June 19	12	9	8	29
June 20	12	9	11	32
June 21	6	8	7	21
June 22	6	5	5	16
June 23	12	7	8	27
June 24	9	6	9	24
June 25	15	7	9	31
June 26	12	9	11	32
June 27	8	11	9	28
June 28	7	7	7	21
June 29	13	13	11	37
June 30	8	13	8	29
Total	181	157	153	491

$X^2 = 13.39$, d.f. $= 32$, N.S.

devoted to commercials. This computation was assisted by the use of network newscast transcripts and the Television News Index and Abstracts.[13] The percentage of news time devoted to TWA stories by day was computed as a ratio of TWA story time and news hole time.

Intercoder reliability estimates were obtained for story type and story topic. Two judges independently coded a random sample of twenty TWA hostage stories. The reliability estimates obtained from this procedure were 90 percent for story type and 90 percent for story topic.

RESULTS

The network evening news broadcasts devoted extensive coverage to the TWA hostage crisis. A total of 491 hostage stories were broadcast over the seventeen-day crisis period, comprising approximately twelve hours of news time. Table 1 lists the total number of hostage reports broadcast on each evening news program during each day of the crisis. ABC's evening newscast reported the largest number of hostage stories, 181, compared to 157 stories by CBS and 153 by NBC. The data show that the amount of coverage given the crisis among the networks was similar from one day to the next ($p<0.001$). These findings are consistent with those reported in earlier analyses of network coverage of the Iranian hostage crisis.

In terms of story type, TWA hostage stories were most frequently anchor

Table 2. Network Hostage Reports by Story Type (Percent)

STORY TYPE	ABC	CBS	NBC
Anchor	49.7 (90)	47.8 (75)	49.7 (76)
Reporter	40.3 (73)	43.3 (68)	41.2 (63)
Commentary/			
Analysis	9.9 (18)	8.9 (14)	9.2 (14)
Total (N = 491)	181	157	153

Table 3. Origin of Network Hostage Reports (Percent)

ORIGIN	ABC	CBS	NBC
Washington/New York	65.7	63.1	67.3
USA/Other	5.0	5.1	5.2
Beirut/Lebanon	12.7	10.2	16.3
London/Other	16.0	17.8	11.1
Location Not Given	.6	3.8	0.0
Total	181	157	153

stories. However, Table 2 indicates that hostage stories presented by the reporter were also frequent. Approximately half of the news items presented by all three networks were anchor stories, whereas only 9 percent of the items involved commentary or analysis. Again the evidence suggests consonance in the nature of the news content devoted to the hostage crisis.

The overwhelming majority of hostage stories were filed from Washington and New York. Over 65 percent of the stories originated from these two national network headquarters. Table 3 shows that Beirut was the third most frequent place of origin for reports on the crisis. Thirteen percent of hostage stories originated from the Lebanese capital.

TOPICAL EMPHASIS

Among the seventeen topics used in the analysis, Hostage Status and U.S. Government Reaction most frequently involved stories on the TWA hijacking. Table 4 lists the number of reports involving each topic. The category Hostage Status accounted for 34 percent of all hostage stories, whereas U.S. Government Reaction accounted for almost 17 percent. The topics Hostage Families, Israel Diplomacy, and Terrorist Demands/Activities also received emphasis in the network evening news reports. The evidence again suggested homogeneity in the topical emphasis of network evening news programs.

Table 4. Network Hostage Reports by Story Topic

TOPIC	ABC	CBS	NBC	TOTAL
Hostage Status	58	62	48	168
U.S. Government Reaction	30	23	30	83
Israel Diplomacy	18	15	11	44
Terrorist Demands/Acts	14	9	14	37
Hostage Families	15	6	13	34
Retaliation Options	14	9	10	33
Nabih Berri/Mediation	8	10	4	22
Airport Security	3	6	8	17
Syria Mediation	6	3	4	13
Citizen Reaction/Media	7	6	1	14
Kidnapped Seven	0	5	2	7
Lebanon: Internal Problems	1	0	4	5
U.S./Israel Diplomacy	2	1	1	4
Private Diplomacy	0	0	1	1
Islam/Culture	2	2	0	4
Lebanon: External Problems	2	0	2	4
World Reaction	1	0	0	1
Total	181	157	153	491

$X^2 = 38.54$, d.f. = 32, N.S.

NEWS TIME DEVOTED TO THE HOSTAGE CRISIS

An average of 14 minutes per newscast was devoted to hostage-crisis stories over the 17-day period. In addition, an average of about 9.6 news items on the crisis were featured in each of the 51 newscasts. Table 5 lists the news time (in minutes) given hostage reports for each day of the crisis. In parentheses on the right is the percentage of newscast time (news hole time) consumed by hostage stories on each of the 17 days examined. These data indicate once more that hostage coverage comprised large proportions of newscast time throughout the crisis period. The data also show that the proportions of the news hole consumed by hostage reports were similar among the evening news programs.

DISCUSSION

A comprehensive visual analysis of network evening news reports broadcast during the TWA hostage crisis indicated that crisis coverage was extensive and continuous. The findings suggested that the hostage crisis was the dominant news event covered over the study period. Most hostage stories

Table 5. Minutes of Network Hostage Reports by Day

NEWSCAST DAY	ABC	CBS	NBC
June 14	10.7 (50.3)	10 (46.7)	12.5 (58.6)
June 15	14.6 (70)	14.7 (68.3)	14.5 (55.3)
June 16	17.6 (94.9)	19 (89.8)	15.8 (73.4)
June 17	19.1 (89.5)	19.2 (88.6)	15.8 (75.4)
June 18	19.9 (91)	14.7 (67.5)	16.6 (76.7)
June 19	20.6 (95.8)	7.6 (35.2)	13.0 (61.4)
June 20	17 (77.9)	17.5 (84.2)	18.1 (86.6)
June 21	14.3 (66)	11.2 (51.5)	10.6 (49)
June 22	10.2 (48.7)	6.9 (32.2)	6.0 (42.6)
June 23	9.5 (46.9)	11.6 (53.6)	15.2 (70.7)
June 24	13.9 (64.6)	9.3 (43)	12.1 (55.9)
June 25	14.9 (67.6)	8.2 (37.6)	13.2 (63.7)
June 26	19.2 (90)	13.6 (62.1)	13.7 (65.4)
June 27	15.0 (68.6)	14.4 (65.6)	14.1 (65.9)
June 28	13.5 (63.8)	14.3 (54)	11.6 (54)
June 29	17.6 (84.2)	19.2 (87.9)	16.3 (76.6)
June 30	12.8 (95.2)	22.3 (97.8)	15.9 (79.6)
Total	260.4	233.7	235

Total Hostage Story Time: 729.1 Minutes

were anchor reports originating from Washington or New York. Topics that most often involved hostage stories were those concerned with the plight of the hostages and U.S. government reactions to the crisis. Little attention was focused on less dramatic topics such as the history of Lebanon and conditions that may have given rise to the TWA hijacking.

These findings strongly indicate that TWA crisis coverage on network evening newscasts was dramatic, reactive, and extensive. This trend in crisis reporting is similar to that portrayed in network evening news accounts of the Iranian hostage crisis. Limited reporting on factors that may have given rise to the crisis suggests that the broadcasts could have played a greater role as interpreter and educator in this instance.

The large proportion of news time devoted to the crisis on the three news broadcasts raises the issue of balance in reporting news of the day. The dominant play that the hostage crisis received might have influenced the issue priorities of newscast viewers. Future research should explore the extent (if any) to which newscast crisis coverage influences the issue agendas of viewers and their perceptions of reality.

NOTES

1. Walter Laqueur, *Terrorism: A Study of National and International Political Violence* (Boston: Little, Brown 1977).

2. Yonah Alexander, "Terrorism, the Media and the Police," *Journal of International Affairs* 32 (Spring-Summer 1978): 101–113.

3. William C. Adams, *Television Coverage of International Affairs* (Norwood, N.J.: Ablex Publishing, 1982).

4. Donald L. Shaw and Maxwell E. McCombs, *Emergence of American Political Issues: The Agenda-Setting Function of the Press* (St. Paul: West, 1977).

5. David L. Altheide, "Three-in-One News: Network Coverage of Iran," *Journalism Quarterly* 59 (Autumn 1982): 482–486.

6. Milan D. Meeske and Mohamad H. Javaheri, "Network Television Coverage of the Iranian Hostage Crisis," *Journalism Quarterly* 59 (Winter 1982): 641–645.

7. David L. Altheide, "Impact of Format and Ideology on TV News Coverage of Iran," *Journalism Quarterly* 62 (Summer 1985): 346–351.

8. Dan Nimmo and James E. Combs, *Nightly Horrors: Crisis Coverage by Television Network News* (Knoxville: University of Tennessee Press, 1985), p. 165.

9. David L. Paletz, John Z. Ayanian, and Peter A. Fozzard, "Terrorism on TV News: The IRA, the FALN, and the Red Brigades," in William C. Adams, ed., *Television Coverage of International Affairs* (Norwood, N.J.: Ablex Publishing, 1982), pp. 143–165.

10. Joseph S. Fowler and Stuart W. Showalter, "Evening Network News Selection: A Confirmation of News Judgment," *Journalism Quarterly* 51 (Winter 1974): 712–715.

11. Nimmo and Combs, *Nightly Horrors*, p. 165.

12. Altheide, "Three-in-One News."

13. Vanderbilt Television News Archive, "Television News Index and Abstracts: A Guide to the Videotape Collection of the Network Evening News Programs in the Vanderbilt Television News Archive" (Nashville: Joint University Libraries, 1985).

2 | Symbolic Functions of Violence and Terror

George Gerbner, University of Pennsylvania

Most of what we know, or think we know, we do not personally experience. Perhaps the most distinguishing characteristic of our species is that for all practical purposes we live in a world we erect through the stories we tell.

Violence and terror have a special role to play in this great storytelling process. They depict social forces in conflict. They dramatize threats to human integrity and the social order. They demonstrate power to lash out, provoke, intimidate, and control. They designate winners and losers in an inescapably political game.

These are all symbolic functions, the focus of my essay. I am not discussing acts of hurting and killing but of the selective and synthetic media re-creations of these acts and of the sociopolitical functions of these re-creations. In so doing I will draw on research of our own as well as of others I have summarized in a report for UNESCO (Gerbner, 1988).

My argument, in brief, is that symbolic uses benefit those who control them. They are usually states and media establishments, not small-scale or isolated actors or insurgents. Though perpetrators of small-scale acts of violence and terror may occasionally force media attention and, in that sense, seem to advance their cause, in the last analysis such a challenge serves to enhance media credibility ("just reporting the facts") and is used to mobilize support for repression often in the form of wholesale state violence and terror or military action, presented as justified by the provocation.

The highly selective and politically shaped portrayals of violence and terror conceal rather than reveal the actual incidence and distribution of real violence and terror. These portrayals, including the choice of labels, serve as projective devices that isolate acts and people from meaningful contexts and set them up to be stigmatized and victimized.

Stigma is a mark of disgrace that evokes disgraceful behavior. Calling some people barbarians makes it easier to act barbarically toward them. Presuming some people to be criminals permits dealing with them in ways otherwise considered criminal. Labeling a large group terrorists seems to justify terrorizing them. Declaring nations enemies makes it legitimate to attack and kill them. Calling some people crazy or insane makes it possible to suspend rules of rationality and decency. Stigma brands deviation from the norm as not only unusual and perhaps unjustified but as evil and sinful. It is one way a culture has to enforce its norms.

The persons stigmatized are the obvious targets, but the real victim of the process is a community's ability to think rationally and creatively about injustice.

The context in which this type of demonstration and socialization goes on is the historically unprecedented mass ritual of television violence and its cultivation of an inequitable sense of power and vulnerability. For the first time in human history we have manufactured a compelling symbolic environment not of the family, the neighborhood, the school, the church, and the selectively used print and film media but the mass ritual of television. It presents a world which, especially in prime time, is largely power-oriented. Its action dramas are by far the major sources of vivid images about violence and terror most people absorb daily beginning with infancy. News by and large has to compete in a marketplace of these dramatic appeals and preconceptions.

Prime time is a world in which men outnumber women three to one. Young people and old people and minorities have less than their share not only of representation but also of opportunities and power, but more than their share of vulnerability and victimization. Violence and terror perform the tasks of the unequal distribution of power. That is their symbolic function.

The typical viewer sees every week an average of twenty-one criminals (including "terrorists," domestic and foreign). Arrayed against them are forty-one public and private law enforcers. (If they live so long, there are also an average of fourteen doctors, six nurses, six lawyers, and two judges to deal with them.) Violence occurs an average of six times per hour in prime time, and over twenty times per hour in weekend daytime children's programming. We absorb an average of two entertaining murders a night. Neither fictional nor factual (news) violence and terror bear much relationship to their actual occurrence in our communities and the world. But they do cultivate an accommodation to the structure of power. Our research on television found that exposure to the pattern of media violence cultivates a differential sense of vulnerability and stigmatization, placing heavier burdens on selected minorities and nationalities.

This is the general context of pervasive and inescapable violent representations within which the labeling and depiction of terrorism and terrorists play out their symbolic social functions.

*   *   *

Much of the controversy over press coverage of terrorism revolves around who should control the news, authorities or media. The contest is reminiscent of the symbiotic relationship of cooperation and conflict between the medieval state and church, in which the church usually emerged as the more credible cultural arm of society, at least until the coming of mass media. Liberal democracies, and even other states, tend to come to similar conclusions concerning the media. The Prevention of Terrorism Act, for example, was enacted in the United Kingdom in the wake of an IRA bombing in 1974 that killed 21 people and injured over 160. The act suspends civil liberties for anyone suspected of supporting the IRA terrorism or withholding information about it. Under its provisions, the police seized a copy of a fifteen-minute untransmitted film shot by a BBC crew at an incident at Carrickmore. After a long debate in Parliament and in the press, the government decided not to prosecute the BBC, but rules on reporting terroristic acts were tightened.

Comparative studies of terrorist labeling and coverage reveal unreliable statistics and blatantly political uses. Although the media in the United States continued to put increasing emphasis on international terrorism throughout the 1970s, the authoritative chronology of transnational terrorism by Mickolus (1980) showed that the frequency of incidents peaked in 1972 with 480 that year and subsequently declined to an average of 340 per year. Many of the reports focused, and still focus, on the Middle East. There has been no comparable coverage of prevalent state and antistate terrorism in many countries of Africa, Latin America, and Asia.

While the physical casualties of highly publicized terrorist acts have been relatively few, the political and military consequences have been far-reaching. The fate of governments, relations among states, scientific exchanges, tourism, and trade have been affected. International tensions, domestic repression, and support for counterviolence have increased. For example, although less than 1 percent of all casualties of international terrorism in 1985 were American, they prompted the forcing down of an Egyptian airliner and the bombing of Tripoli (probably based, as it turned out, on faulty intelligence).

Although international terrorism by and against states received most attention, Bassiouni (1981, 1982) and others pointed out that terrorist acts in a national context far outnumber international ones. Disappearances, bombings, kidnappings, and state violence in many countries, often unreported, claim thousands of times more victims than do well-publicized acts of international terror.

Wurth-Hough (1983) documented the role of media coverage of terrorism in selecting events and defining issues for the public. Paletz, Fozzard, and Ayanian (1982) analyzed *New York Times* coverage of the IRA, the Red Brigades, and the Fuerzas Armadas de Liberación Nacional (FALN) from July 1, 1977, to June 30, 1979, and found no basis for the charge that coverage legitimizes the cause of terrorist organizations. On the contrary, 70 percent of the stories mentioned neither the cause nor the objectives of the terrorists; almost 75 percent mentioned neither the organization nor its supporters; and the 7 percent that did mention names surrounded them with statements issued by authorities.

In a follow-up study of U.S. network news, Milburn et al. (1987) also noted the frequent omission of any causal explanation for terrorist acts and the attribution of mental instability to terrorists and their leaders. (Similar acts directed against countries other than the United States were more frequently explained.) The implication, the researchers noted, was that "you can't negotiate with crazy people."

Knight and Dean (1982) provided a detailed account of how the Canadian press coverage of the siege and recapturing of the Iranian embassy in London from Arab nationalist "gunmen" served to assert the efficiency and legitimacy of violence by the British Special Forces. In the process of transforming crime and punishment into a selectively choreographed newsworthy event, the media "have to some extent assumed the functions of moral and political—in short, ideological—reproduction performed previously (and limitedly) by the visibility of the public event itself." It is not accidental, the authors claimed, that highly publicized and "morally coherent" scenarios of violence and terror have made public punishment unnecessary as demonstrations of state ideology and power.

Typically isolated from their historical and social context, denied description of conditions or cause, and portrayed as unpredictable and irrational, if not insane (see, for example, Milburn et al., 1987), those labeled terrorists symbolize a menace that rational, humane, and democratic means cannot reach or control. In a domestic context of racial violence, Paletz and Dunn (1969) studied the effects of news coverage of urban riots and concluded that the attempt to present a view acceptable to most readers failed to illuminate the conditions in the black communities that led to the riots. News of civil disturbance shares with coverage of terrorist activity the tendency to cultivate a pervasive sense of fear and danger, and of the consequent acceptability of harsh measures to combat it.

De Boer (1979) summarized survey results in five countries and found that although terrorists claimed relatively few victims, the media coverage cultivated a sense of imminent danger that only unusual steps could overcome. Terrorism was considered a "very serious" problem by nine out of ten Americans and nearly as many British respondents. Six out of ten people in the Federal Republic of Germany considered it "the most important public event of the year."

Six or seven out of ten respondents in the United States, the United Kingdom, and the Federal Republic of Germany favored the introduction of the death penalty for terrorists. Similar majorities approved using a "special force" that would hunt down and kill terrorists in any country; placing them "under strict surveillance, even though our country might then somewhat resemble a police state;" using "extra stern and harsh action" unlike against other criminals; and "limitations of personal rights by such measures as surveillance and house searches" in order to "combat terrorism."

Eight out of ten Germans in the Federal Republic approved a news embargo instituted after a kidnapping, and six out of ten thought that conversations between the accused and their lawyers should be monitored to prevent new acts of terrorism.

From one-fifth to over half of the respondents in the Federal Republic of Germany said that "one has to be careful" of what one says to avoid being considered sympathetic to terrorists. Sympathizers were considered to be those who oppose the death penalty, who believe their "lawyers have the right at all times to visit terrorists in prison," who think their "criticisms of our society to be justified in some respects," or who feel pity for them.

*   *   *

Psychological research on individual aggression and violence has been the most widely publicized. It has also been relatively easy to refute. Critics of aggression research point to the difficulty of relating experiments to real-life situations, question the validity of relating aggressive tendencies to actual violence, and charge that blaming most individual aggression or violence on the media distracts attention from underlying social influences and the greater threat of collective, official, organized, and legitimated violence. They recall Friedrich Schiller's complaint: "It is criminal to steal a purse, daring to steal a fortune, a mark of greatness to steal a crown. The blame diminishes as the guilt increases."

Indeed, most research on the effects of violence has been generated by fears that violence and terror in the media brutalize children and undermine the social order. While that may be partly true (and a non sequitur), seldom asked and rarely publicized have been broader questions of policy: Why should media organizations, established institutions of society, undermine their existence by promoting violence? Are incitation and imitation really the principal consequences of exposure to violence? Are there consequences that may benefit media institutions and their sponsors? If so, what are they? Can they help explain the persistence of media policies despite public criticism and international embarrassment over flooding many cultures with images of violence and terror?

The conventional debate between those who fear imitation and those who claim popular demand begs the point. Although conflict is essential and violence is legitimate in news and drama, there is no evidence of popular demand for violence per se. Perhaps one or two out of the ten highest-rated television programs are violent shows. Most television (and news) violence are formula-bound, cheap to produce, "travel" better than other fare, have a minimal attention value, and can thus be profitable commodities despite their mediocre ratings.

It is clear that violence-inspired mayhem poses no threat to modern societies. On the contrary, the violence-terror scenario, as circuses of old, may function to isolate and annihilate, or at least control such threats.

The research evidence suggests that prolonged exposure to stories and scenes of violence and terror can mobilize aggressive tendencies, can desensitize some and isolate others, can trigger violence in a few and intimidate the many. But lawlessness and massive disorder relate more to illicit commerce, wars, unemployment, and other social trends than to the violence index we have been compiling since 1967. Small-scale terrorists have toppled no state without a collapse of power from other causes; mostly they have provoked reprisals, repression, and an excuse for invasions.

It may well be that a media system strikes an implicit balance between the costs and benefits of the violence scenario. On one hand, there is the cost of public anxiety, and accommodation to injustice and inhumanity. On the other hand is the less visible but historically and empirically demonstrable gain in power—personal and institutional—derived from the ability to depersonalize enemies; to cultivate vulnerability and dependence in subordinates; to achieve instant support for swift and tough measures at home and abroad in what is presented as an exceedingly mean and scary world. The scenario provides its producers with the sense and reality of power, and its persistence may be understood, among other things, in terms of its utility for those who define and control its uses.

REFERENCES

Bassiouni, M. Cherif. "Terrorism, Law Enforcement, and the Mass Media: Perspectives, Problems, Proposals." *Journal of Criminal Law and Criminology* 72, no. 1 (1981).

Bassiouni, M. Cherif. "Media Coverage of Terrorism: The Law and the Public." *Journal of Communication* 33, no. 2 (1982): 128–143.

DeBoer, Connie. "The Polls: Terrorism and Hijacking." *Public Opinion Quarterly* 43 (Fall 1979): 410–418.

Gerbner, George. "Violence and Terror in the Mass Media." *Reports and Papers in Mass Communication,* no. 102. Paris: Unesco, 1988.

Knight, Graham, and Tony Dean. "Myth and the Structure of News." *Journal of Communication* 32, no. 2 (1982): 144–161.

Mickolus, Edward F. *Transnational Terrorism: A Chronology of Events, 1986–1979.* Westport, Conn: Greenwood Press, 1980.

Milburn, Michael A., Claudia Bowley, Janet Fay-Dumaine, and Debbie Ann Kennedy. "An Attributional Analysis of the Media Coverage of Terrorism." Paper presented at the 10th Annual Meeting of the International Society of Political Psychology, San Francisco, July 6, 1987.

Paletz, David L., Peter A. Fozzard, and John Z. Ayanian. "The I.R.A., the Red Brigades and the F.A.L.N. in the *New York Times.*" *Journal of Communication* 32, no. 2 (1982): 162–171.

———, and Robert Dunn. "Press Coverage of Civil Disorders: A Case Study of Winston-Salem." *Public Opinion Quarterly* 33, no. 3 (1969): 328–345.

Wurth-Hough, Sandra. "Network News Coverage of Terrorism: The Early Years." *Terrorism* 6, no. 3 (1983): pp. 403–521.

3 | News Coverage as the Contagion of Terrorism: Dangerous Charges Backed by Dubious Science

Robert Picard, Emerson College

When NBC News broadcast a three-and-a-half-minute interview in May 1986 with Abul (Mohammed) Abbas, head of the Palestine Liberation Front that hijacked the *Achille Lauro* in 1985, the news organization was subjected to swift and pointed criticism. "Terrorism thrives on this kind of publicity," charged State Department spokesman Charles Redman. He said it "encourages the terrorist activities we're all seeking to deter."[1]

A similar response was seen in Great Britain when the British government attacked the BBC for its plans to broadcast the documentary "Real Lives: At the Edge of the Union," which included an interview with Martin McGuinness, a spokesman for the legal political wing of the Irish Republican Army who is accused of being a top-ranking official in the outlawed paramilitary group. Home Secretary Leon Brittan asked the BBC not to air the program, saying it was "wholly contrary to the public interest."[2]

Such incidents have led to calls for more control over what is broadcast and printed about terrorism and those who engage in such political violence. At the American Bar Association meeting in London in 1985, Prime Minister Margaret Thatcher told the gathered attorneys that democracies "must find a way to starve the terrorists and hijackers of the oxygen of publicity on which they depend."[3] Her statement met with support from U.S. Attorney General Edwin Meese and other U.S. officials.

While these efforts have been aimed at getting the media to adhere to voluntary guidelines, other individuals have suggested that legal restraints be imposed. Imposition of such restraints would face greater difficulty in the U.S. than abroad, due to the First Amendment, but many argue they are necessary to control terrorism and protect public safety.

Behind the efforts to induce self-restraints or impose government restraints on the media is the belief that coverage of terrorism and terrorists creates more terrorism and terrorists. The idea that the media are the contagion of terrorism has been widely heralded and is repeatedly used to justify efforts to alter media coverage. This has occurred despite the fact that there is no significant evidence that media acts as a contagion.

This paper will review the argument that media coverage spreads terror-

100

ism by giving encouragement to those who engage in such violence and explore the literature upon which it is based. It will also suggest paradigms within which to view and explore media effects on terrorists that offer a variety of important research opportunities.

THE CONTAGION LITERATURE

During the past two decades, the literature associating the media with terrorism and implicating the media as a contagion of such violence has grown rapidly. When carefully dissecting that literature, however, one finds it contains no credible evidence that media are an important factor in inducing and diffusing terrorist acts.

Most books, articles, essays, and speeches on the topic are comprised of sweeping generalities, conjecture, supposition, anecdotal evidence based on dubious correlations, and endless repetition of equally weak arguments and nonscientific evidence offered by other writers on the subject of terrorism.

As one reviews the literature, it becomes shockingly clear that not a single study based on accepted social science research methods has established a cause-effect relationship between media coverage and the spread of terrorism. Yet public officials, scholars, editors, reporters, and columnists continually link the two elements and present their relationship as proven.

The dearth of evidence associating the two variables is not the result of conflicting studies or arguments over interpretation of evidence, but rather the inexplicable absence of research on the subject. At times some scholars have attempted to overcome that problem or to place the pallor of respectability over their opinions by "borrowing" conclusions from the literature of the effects of televised violence and crime on viewers and then projecting similar effects to coverage of terrorism.

The use of this questionable tactic is disquieting to anyone who ascribes to social science research philosophy. It is especially disturbing when one considers the potential abrogation of civil liberties that could result and the unsettled state of knowledge about the effects of televised violence and crime.

Without wishing to cast aspersions on mediated violence research, it is safe to say that, in the aggregate, the thousands of studies on the subject are contradictory, inconclusive, and based on widely differing definitions, methods, and assumptions. The literature has been the subject of some of the most heated debate in the social sciences.

Social learning, arousal, and disinhibition theories on the effects of media portrayals and violence and crime have nevertheless been transferred to the issue of terrorism portrayal. The results of studies supporting the views of terrorism researchers have been accepted in the face of conflicting evidence.

This has occurred despite the fact that studies on the effects of portrayals of violence and crime have yielded no cause-effect relationship. At best, it can be said that media portrayals do not cause the audience to become violent but *may* affect *some* media users who have antisocial tendencies and spread uncertainty and fear among others.

Although these violence-research findings suggest reasonable hypotheses for terrorism research, no research along those lines has been conducted. Instead, what should only be hypotheses about media and terrorism have been accepted as fact.

Some of the more fascinating pseudoscientific evidence offered in support of the notion that media are the contagion, reported in some of the most important sources on media and terrorism, are public opinion polls of political and law enforcement officials, as well as members of the public, about the relationship between media and terrorism.

While the polls present interesting insights into the perceptions of these individuals at given times, and add something to the understanding of how terrorism affects people, they are used by some writers as evidence that media are indeed the contagion of terrorism. Because the public and officials believe them to be the contagion, media must be the culprit, we are told.

Because the opinion of these groups of people is presumably affected by the agenda set by the past statements of government officials, media critics, and terrorism-control researchers—all of whom have repeatedly alleged the link between media and terrorism—it is not surprising that other officials and the public should parrot their views.

Despite such problems, the contagion argument is continually used against media. Rudolf Levy, a Defense Department expert on terrorism who has taught at the U.S. Army Intelligence Center and School, recently conveyed the media-as-contagion view throughout the military community in the publication *Military Intelligence,* saying:

Experts believe that this type of coverage often has adverse effects, such as:

- Encouraging the formation of new groups. Tactical successes and successful exploitation of the media lead to terrorists taking advantage of the momentum of previous actions and, thus, to an increase in terrorist acts.

- Keeping the terrorist organization's name before the public and "the masses" on whose behalf the terrorists supposedly act.

- Leading other less successful groups or individuals to commit more daring acts of terrorist violence.

- Tempting terrorists, who have received favorable media coverage in the past, to attempt to seize control of the media.[4]

A similar view has been expressed by the American Legal Foundation, a right-wing group that recently urged the government to restrict media coverage. The group argues that "because they give the terrorists a convenient stage to vent their political grievances, the media actually encourage terrorism and may promote the increasing violence and drama of terrorist attacks."[5]

Some of the most recognizable names in terrorism research are less sanguine about the accuracy of the contagion hypothesis, but they have nevertheless embraced and/or diffused it widely. For example, M. Cherif Bassiouni, who has written widely on the subject and taught many who are carrying on research and activities aimed at preventing or controlling political violence through legal means, recognizes the problems with the contagion idea but nevertheless does not reject it. "Although this hypothesis would not appear entirely susceptible to empirical verification, at least with respect to ideologically motivated individuals, concern over this contagion effect has been repeatedly expressed, and the theory retains a certain intuitive reasonableness," he wrote.[6]

Other experts such as Alex Schmid and Janny de Graaf at the Center for the Study of Social Conflicts in the Netherlands are willing to accept the contagion effect despite the lack of empirical evidence that it exists or that it would not exist if the media coverage were removed. Although admitting gaps in knowledge about the contagion effect, they still argue:

> The most serious effect of media reporting on insurgent terrorism, however, is the likely increase in terroristic activities. The media can provide the potential terrorist with all the ingredients that are necessary to engage in this type of violence. They can reduce inhibitions against the use of violence, they can offer models and know-how to potential terrorists and they can motivate them in various ways.[7]

Robert L. Rabe, assistant chief of police for the Metropolitan Police Department in Washington, D.C., promoted the view that there may be value in the hypotheses as well. In his address at a terrorism conference, he stated:

> And what of the contagion of such detailed coverage of a terrorist incident? By glorifying terrorist activities with extensive news coverage, the event is projected as an attraction for others to emulate. If such is the case, terrorism has truly made the television media a pawn in the great game of propaganda.[8]

Even members of the media have accepted the contagion idea. NBC News President Larry Grossman recently presented that view in a more popular form to a Society of Professional Journalists' meeting. "Does television allow itself to be 'used' by terrorists and does television coverage, therefore, encourage terrorist acts? The answer is yes to both," he said. "The very existence of television undoubtedly bears some responsibility for the 'copycat' syndrome of terrorism today."[9]

But not all terrorism scholars fully embrace the view. Brian Jenkins, director of the Rand Corporation's terrorism research, has argued that the media cannot be solely blamed for the spread of terrorism. "The news media are responsible for terrorism to about the same extent that commercial aviation is responsible for airline hijackings," he says. "The vast communications network that makes up the news media is simply another vulnerability in a technologically advanced and free society."[10]

Although there has never been a scientifically based study on the contagion effect of media coverage per se, several related contagion studies have been conducted and are of interest. The most significant study has been conducted by Midlarsky, Crenshaw, and Yoshida, who sought to answer the question of why terroristic acts spread across nations in Western Europe and Latin America. Using the theory of hierarchy, the authors attempt to explain the spread of terrorism among the nations. In the case of Western Europe, the authors found that "terrorism spread from the least powerful to the most powerful, from the weak states to the strong."[11]

The Midlarsky study found that European terrorist groups, for example, borrowed ideology, rhetoric, and methods from the Third World. The biggest contagion effect was found in the transfers of the technique of bombing in both Latin America and Europe, with kidnappings most significant in Latin America and hijacking to a lesser extent there. Media were never mentioned as a cause of the diffusion of terrorist techniques.

Security adviser Edward Heyman and CIA researcher Edward Mickolus later disputed the full findings of the Midlarsky study, citing inadequacies in its data base and some of its inferences, but they did not dispute its general concept. The two argued that their own research indicated that two noncontagion diffusion factors were important in the spread of violence: extensive intergroup cooperation and the idea of transporting terrorist acts to locations where they could best be carried out. They argued that transportation was the biggest factor. Again, no mention of media coverage was made as being an important cause of the spread of terrorism.[12]

Rand Corporation studies have found some evidence of contagion in the diffusion process of terrorist activity types. Jenkins, although unwilling to completely damn news coverage as the culprit, has noted clusters of occurrences in airline hijackings and embassy sieges and indicated that media *might* have played a role in those occurrences.[13] The inference, however, is based on no scientific evidence.

Other research on terrorism has noted that in the case of many airline hijackings in the 1970s, for example, terrorist hijackers often had specific knowledge of radio, navigation, and operating equipment on aircraft and of commercial aviation practices, suggesting they had specialized training and that extensive planning of campaigns of hijacking had occurred. These factors tend to indicate that some of the multiple hijackings were planned well in advance and that the "clustering" of hijacking may not necessarily be blamed on media coverage alone.

DIFFUSION THEORY POSSIBILITIES

General conclusions that can be drawn from studies of diffusion of innovations in other situations do not provide much support for the view that media are crucial elements as a contagion. Mass media have been found to be best at assisting diffusion when combined with interpersonal channels and when used in reinforcing rather than persuasive roles. These findings are consistent with and an outgrowth of the two-step flow theory research of Lazarsfeld and Katz and others who have shown that interpersonal influences are much stronger than media in altering attitudes and behavior.[14] This interpersonal influence approach arose in the 1940s as social scientists were forced to reject the stimulus-response-based theories of media effects offered in the 1930s. Those theories placed media influences on individuals very high, but were not supported by scientific research.

If one accepts general diffusion theory as having relevance to the spread of terrorism, one would have to hypothesize that media may play a role in the awareness aspect of the adoption process of terrorism, but only a minor part—at best—in the evaluative, acceptance, and adoption portions of the diffusion of terrorist techniques.

Diffusion principles also provide a testable explanation for the increasing number of acts of political violence. Because they provide an established normal S-curve of cumulative adoption of innovations, researchers on terrorism could develop methods to analyze adoption of various techniques and practices to determine whether the adoption followed normal patterns or was unusual.

I do not wish to fall into the trap of using the evidence from diffusion research as conclusive evidence about the role of the media in terrorism, as many terrorism researchers have done by accepting results from violence research. The general conclusions drawn from diffusion research, however, have not been the subject of the heated debate that has surrounded the violence research because they have been much less contradictory and inconclusive. The diffusion principles suggest hypotheses that are well suited for testing in the realm of terrorism, although no such studies exist today that add evidence to the discussion of media and terrorism.[15]

It is clear, then, that no causal link has been established using any acceptable social science research methods between media coverage and the spread of terrorism. Without such a link, the media are being unjustifiably blamed for the increasing acts of violence throughout the world.

I do not wish to be interpreted, however, as taking the position that no link can ever be established, only that one cannot do so with the state of knowledge today. The fact that the media cannot be shown to be the contagion of terrorism does not exonerate it from excesses in coverage that have been shown to harm authorities' ability to cope with specific incidents of violence, have endangered the lives of victims and authorities, have been unduly sensational, and have spread fear among the public. For such errors in judgment and violations of existing industry standards, the offending media must bear the responsibility. One would hope that such problems will diminish as journalists become more acquainted with the techniques of terrorists and discuss the problems and implications of their coverage.

COVERAGE AS A PREVENTATIVE OF TERRORISM

If the media cannot be shown to be the cause of the spread of terrorism, can they be shown to be useful in preventing or reducing the scale of violence in terrorist attacks?

One important school of thought suggests coverage may actually reduce the possibility of future violent action on the part of those who engage in terroristic violence by removing the need for individuals and groups to resort to violence in order to gain coverage. The view that some coverage may reduce terrorism is not held solely at the fringes of the terrorism research community, although it receives little support among government officials and those to whom they most often turn for advice in combating terrorism.

Abraham H. Miller, who has written extensively on legal issues involving the media during terrorist incidents, notes the major elements of the view: "If terrorism is a means of reaching the public forum, violence can be defused by providing accessibility to the media without the necessity of an entry fee of blood and agony," he writes.[16] Indeed, that was a conclusion reached at a conference on terrorism at Ditchley Castle in Oxfordshire, England, in 1978.

Another conclusion urging full, complete, and serious media coverage of such violence was reached by the Task Force on Terrorism and Disorders, which noted that

> the media can be most influential in setting the tone for a proper response by the civil authorities to disorders, acts of terrorism, and political violence. It can provide an outlet for the expression of legitimate public concern on important issues so as to act as a safety valve, and it can bring pressure to bear in response to public sentiment in an effective manner to redress grievances and to change official policies.[17]

The response to the problem of terrorism should be more, not less, news coverage, the task force argued: "The news media should devote more, rather than less, space and attention to the phenomena of extraordinary violence."[18] If such coverage avoids glamorizing the perpetrators of violence, provides reliable information, and gives appropriate emphasis to the consequences of violence, it will increase public understanding, reduce public fear, and assist in reducing violence, the report indicated.

These conclusions were reached by the task force despite the fact that it generally accepted a stimulus-response view of media effects. While admitting that no authoritative evidence directly linked media and violence, the group accepted the premises that media directly or indirectly influence potential perpetrators of violence and potential victims and that coverage of such violence affects the ability of authorities to respond.

If one accepts the view that unrequited grievances, frustration, and despair lead to political rebellion, and that those who rebel are denied forums in the media because the media are institutions that support and perpetuate the dominant political order of the states in which they operate, one must conclude that normal media channels are regularly denied to these extreme dissidents.

This being the case, the only possible avenues left for gaining a media forum are acts designed to force their way into the forums. Violence, as we are all too painfully aware, is an effective way of achieving such forums.

The provision-of-forums-as-a-means-of-combating-terrorism view holds that reasonable provision of forums in noncoerced environments may help reduce the frustration that leads to such violent acts and lead to an understanding of the issues or points of view of the dissidents. Two psychologists who conduct research in the area of terrorism, Jeffrey Rubin of Tufts University and Nehemia Friedland of Tel Aviv University and the Project on Terrorism at the Jaffee Center of Strategic Studies, recently argued that governments should help provide access, which would be necessary in most nations where broadcasting is government-operated or government-related. The two argued:

> Governments should also try to reduce the destructiveness of terrorism by making it clear that a less dramatic performance will suffice to get the desired audience attention. Cameo appearances, for example, might be invited or encouraged as a substitute for full-scale productions [terrorist theater]. Imagine that Yasir Arafat or George Habash were to be invited to meet the press on Israeli television to express their views on what they consider to be political reality in the Middle East. Such an arrangement would provide these actors with the element of legitimacy they seek and would air issues without resorting to anything more violent than the savagery of the Israeli news media.[19]

As with most of the theories surrounding the role of the media in terrorism, there is little supporting evidence—only intuition—bolstering this free-expression-as-a-means-of-controlling-violence theory. The theory has merit and deserves to be studied closely, however, as do the principles from the diffusion approach.

Several possible studies come to mind here, including behavorial analyses of groups whose views have been carried by media without coercion. In recent times, members of IRA, Palestinian, Basque, Red Army Faction, and other groups have received platforms to express their views through interviews and other forums. A study of the behavior of these groups in the periods after such interviews would be enlightening. One would hypothesize that the behavior would become less spectacularly violent after the forums were provided—a hypothesis borne out by casual observation in the case of Yasir Arafat's supporters since international forums were provided the PLO in the 1970s.

It would appear to be inappropriate for journalists to interview members of groups taking part in terrorist acts while such acts are underway. This type of interview has occurred during the course of hijackings, building sieges, kidnappings, and other prolonged acts of terrorism.

Interviews under such conditions are a direct reward for the specific act of terrorism underway and can interfere with efforts to resolve the crisis. There is also some evidence that such coverage can prolong crises. In addition, such interviews all too often increase the spectacle of the event, spread fear, and provide a coerced platform for the views of the groups involved.

I do not believe, however, that interviews not conducted during a specific event need be treated in the same manner, despite protestations to the contrary by government officials. Interviews such as those of Abul Abbas and Martin McGuinness, mentioned at the beginning of this paper, clearly do not provide a reward for a specific violent act, do not interfere with authorities' efforts to control a specific incident, do not endanger the lives of any hostages or authorities attempting to cope with hostage situations, and obviously cannot prolong a specific crisis when none exists. If the coverage-as-a-preventative-measure theory is correct, such interviews should be helpful.

When such coverage is provided, however, journalists should not allow their media to become mere propaganda vehicles for those who engage in violence. Such occasions should be used as a means of exploring the causes and factors that lead to violence, of discussing policy options, and of encouraging nonviolent alternatives. This means that the journalist must exercise control and judgment in the interview, not allowing the subject of the interview to control the topics covered or the time spent on specific issues. The journalist must steer the subject away from overtly propagandistic statements with probing, serious questions aimed at getting to the heart of the issues; that is, the journalist must truly question the interviewee, not merely provide a forum.

I am not sanguine about the idea of forums being provided to terrorists, however. The idea of opening the media to alienated and disenfranchised persons and groups as a means of reducing violence seems preferable to nearly any other option for controlling violence, but the chances of the idea being widely accepted are very slim. The media themselves would be reluctant to do so out of fear of offending audiences and experiencing revenue losses, as well as fears of being accused of supporting terrorists. A measure of existence of that disapprobation can be seen in the criticism heaped on NBC by other media and journalists after the Abbas interview.

In addition, the media are not likely to convey much information conflicting with the views of the government in the nation in which they operate or that is likely to create a conflict between the media and the government. Philip Schlesinger has noted that the media generally reflect their government's perspectives when covering terrorism—regardless of the type of state in which they exist—and that perspectives that conflict with the government's views are rarely carried.[20]

As a result of such problems, I believe it will be difficult to convince government officials and their terrorism advisers that media may possibly aid the campaign against terrorist violence.

SUMMARY

The lack of scientifically acceptable evidence about the media and terrorism, and the absence of criticism of the scanty and questionable evidence about media effects that is offered by some government officials, security advisers, and researchers leave the media open to significant attacks by legislators and executive agencies.

Because there will be continuing terrorism in the years to come and no projected decline in such activity, there is great danger ahead for the media in all nations that suffer from terrorist attacks. Movement toward restricting the flow of information through the media is gaining momentum, backed by dubious studies couched in the scientific jargon of the social sciences. Most officials and members of the public do not know enough to be able to question that evidence.

Those of us in the social sciences who appreciate and understand the contributions of the media to society have a duty to help the public and officials part the veil of ignorance that shrouds the subject of terrorism and the media. We must help set and undertake a research agenda that can be realistically expected to answer the serious charges and questions about journalism's roles in the spread of terrorism.

I do not mean that we should set out with our own set of biases to "prove" that the media are innocent. But we do need to set out to find out just what the reality is. I suspect we will find that the media are a contributing factor in the spread of terrorism, just as easy international transportation, the easy availability of weapons and explosives, the intransigence of some governments' policies, the provision of funds to terrorists by a variety of supportive governments, and a host of other factors are to blame.

Whatever the results of our research, it will move us closer to reality than the views offered by those who argue that the media are wholly at fault and those who argue that they are blameless. The resulting knowledge will make it less likely that governments will act precipitously to control media coverage and that journalists will gain a better understanding of terrorism that will leave them less open to manipulation and more aware of the consequences of their actions.

NOTES

1. Peter J. Boyer, "Arab's Interview Stirs News Debate," *New York Times,* May 7, 1986, p. A7.

2. Joel Bellmann, "BBC: Clearing the Air," *The Journalist,* January 1986, p. 20.

3. "Thatcher Urges the Press to Help 'Starve' Terrorist," *New York Times,* July 16, 1985, p. A3.

4. Rudolf Levy, "Terrorism and the Mass Media," *Military Intelligence,* October–December, 1985, p. 35.

5. *Terrorism and the Media* (Washington, D.C.: American Legal Foundation, n.d.), p. 24.

6. M. Cherif Bassiouni, "Problems of Media Coverage of Nonstate-Sponsored Terror-Violence Incidents," in Lawrence Z. Freedman and Yonah Alexander, eds., *Perspectives on Terrorism* (Wilmington, Del.: Scholarly Resources, 1983), p. 184.

7. Alex P. Schmid and Janny de Graaf, *Violence as Communication: Insurgent Terrorism and the Western News Media* (Beverly Hills, Calif.: Sage Publications, 1982), p. 142.

8. Robert L. Rabe, "Terrorism and the Media," in Yonah Alexander and Seymour M. Finger, eds., *Terrorism: Interdisciplinary Perspectives* (New York: John Jay Press, 1977), p. 69.

9. Larry Grossman, "The Face of Terrorism," *The Quill,* June 1986, p. 38.

10. Quoted in Schmid and de Graaf, *Violence as Communication,* p. 143.

11. Manus I. Midlarsky, Martha Crenshaw, and Fumihiko Yoshida, "Why Violence Spreads: The Contagion of International Terrorism," *International Studies Quarterly* (June 1980): 276.

12. Edward Heyman and Edward Mickolus, "Observations on 'Why Violence Spreads,' " *International Studies Quarterly* June 1980): 299–305.

13. Brian M. Jenkins, "The Psychological Implications of Media-Covered Terrorism," *The Rand Paper Series* P-6627, June 1981.

14. Paul Lazarsfeld and Elihu Katz, *Personal Influence: The Part Played by People in Mass Communications* (Glencoe, Ill.: Free Press, 1955).

15. An excellent volume drawing together the results of hundreds of diffusion studies throughout the world is Everett M. Rogers, *Communication of Innovations: A Cross-Cultural Approach*, 3d ed. (New York: Free Press, 1983).

16. Abraham H. Miller, *Terrorism: The Media and the Law* (Dobbs Ferry, N.Y.: Transnational Publishers, 1982), p. 24.

17. National Advisory Committee on Criminal Justice Standards and Goals, *Disorders and Terrorism: Report of the Task Force on Disorders and Terrorism* (Washington, D.C.: Law Enforcement Assistance Administration, 1977), p. 65.

18. Ibid., p. 368.

19. Jeffrey Z. Rubin and Nehemia Friedland, "Theater of Terror," *Psychology Today* (March 1986): 28.

20. Philip Schlesinger, Graham Murdock, and Philip Elliot, *Televising 'Terrorism': Political Violence in Popular Culture* (London: Comedia Publishing Group, 1983).

Reprinted from *Political Communication and Persuasion* 3 (Fall 1986): 35–40.

APPENDIX B

Selected Documents

Editor's Note: From the proliferation of documents related to terrorism and the media, we have selected representative material reflecting the views of governments (the United States and Canada), intergovernmental bodies (the Council of Europe), nongovernmental groups (the Task Force), and the media (media guidelines). They are reprinted by permission.

4 | Disorders and Terrorism

*Report of the Task Force on Disorders and Terrorism
(Washington: National Advisory Committee on Criminal
Justice Standards and Goals, 1976).*

A. NEWS AND ENTERTAINMENT MEDIA RESPONSIBILITY FOR THE PREVENTION OF EXTRAORDINARY VIOLENCE

Factual and fictional depictions of incidents of extraordinary violence in the mass media are an important part of the background against which individual choices whether or not to participate in crimes of this nature are made. They also are a significant influence on public fears and expectations. So long as extraordinary violence is a fact of social life, the media cannot and should not avoid portraying and discussing it. But the special responsibility of the mass media in the prevention of extraordinary violence should dictate some guiding principles to govern the presentation of this material. In particular:

1. Factual journalistic coverage of extraordinary violence in the mass media should be as accurate and complete as the availability of information permits. Such coverage should:

   a. Give appropriate emphasis to the immediate and long-term consequences of extraordinary violence, for both victims and perpetrators;
   b. Include reliable information on the capacity of law enforcement agencies to deal with extraordinary violence; and
   c. Avoid unnecessary glamorization of persons who engage in crimes of extraordinary violence.

2. Editorials, features, and journalistic background pieces concerning extraordinary violence should attempt to place the phenomenon in total context, by reference to other problems of law enforcement and to related political and social issues.

3. Particular fictional presentations of extraordinary violence in the entertainment media, and the variety of mass entertainment that has criminal violence as its subject matter, should be crafted so as to:

   a. Avoid giving any general impression that participation in extraordinary violence is a common, glamorous, or effective means of resolving personal or political problems;
   b. Avoid conveying the impression that law enforcement responses

to extraordinary violence are generally either incompetent or
marked by the use of extreme force; and

   c. Present affirmative portrayals of private individuals and officials
coping effectively with extraordinary violence and its consequences.

B. NEWS MEDIA SELF-REGULATION IN CONTEMPORANEOUS COVERAGE OF TERRORISM AND DISORDER

When an incident involving a confrontation between law enforcement
officers and participants in mass disorder, terrorism, or quasi-terrorism is in
progress, the role of the news media is an important and controversial one.
The manner in which information about the incident is collected, and the
form of its presentation to the public, will necessarily affect the conduct of
the agencies and persons involved. In addition, these factors will be critical
influences on the growth or spread, if any, of the incident. Finally, the approach taken by the media to news-gathering and reporting on an incident-
by-incident basis will have an important cumulative effect on public attitudes toward the phenomenon of extraordinary violence, the groups and
persons who participate in it, and the official measures taken against it.

No hard rules can be prescribed to govern media performance during
incidents of extraordinary violence. Whatever principles are adopted must
be generated by the media themselves, out of a recognition of special public
responsibility. But in general, the essence of an appropriate approach to
news-gathering is summarized in the principle of minimum intrusiveness:
representatives of the media should avoid creating any obvious media presence at an incident scene that is greater than that required to collect full,
accurate, and balanced information on the actions of participants and the
official response to them. Similarly, the essence of an appropriate approach
to contemporaneous reporting of extraordinary violence lies in the principle
of complete, noninflammatory coverage; the public is best served by reporting that omits no important detail and that attempts to place all details in
context.

Putting these general principles into practice, however, requires hard
choices for the media, both at the organizational policy level and by the
working reporter. In particular:

   1. News media organizations and representatives wishing to adopt the
principle of minimum intrusiveness in their gathering of news relating
to incidents of extraordinary violence should consider the following
devices, among others:

      a. Use of pool reporters to cover activities at incident scenes or
within police lines;

      b. Self-imposed limitations on the use of high-intensity television lighting, obtrusive camera equipment, and other special news-gathering technologies at incident scenes;

   c. Limitations on media solicitation of interviews with barricaded or hostage-holding suspects and other incident participants;

   d. Primary reliance on officially designated spokesmen as sources of information concerning law enforcement operations and plans; and

   e. Avoidance of inquiries designed to yield tactical information that would prejudice law enforcement operations if subsequently disclosed.

2. News media organizations and representatives wishing to follow the principle of complete, noninflammatory coverage in contemporaneous reporting of incidents of extraordinary violence should consider the following devices, among others:

   a. Delayed reporting of details believed to have a potential for inflammation or aggravation of an incident that significantly outweighs their interest to the general public;

   b. Delayed disclosure of information relating to incident location, when that information is not likely to become public knowledge otherwise and when the potential for incident growth or spread is obviously high;

   c. Delayed disclosure of information concerning official tactical planning that, if known to incident participants, would seriously compromise law enforcement efforts;

   d. Balancing of reports incorporating self-serving statements by incident participants with contrasting information from official sources and with data reflecting the risks that the incident has created to noninvolved persons;

   e. Systematic predisclosure verification of all information concerning incident-related injuries, deaths, and property destruction; and

   f. Avoidance, to the extent possible, of coverage that tends to emphasize the spectacular qualities of an incident or the presence of spectators at an incident scene.

C. FOLLOW-UP REPORTING OF EXTRAORDINARY VIOLENCE BY NEWS MEDIA

Although contemporaneous news-gathering and reporting practices can have great impact on the course of an incident of extraordinary violence and the shape of its eventual resolution, the coverage that the phenomena of extraordinary violence receives during nonemergency periods is ultimately even more significant. From the follow-up reporting of particular incidents and their aftermaths, as well as from general and background reporting, the public at large receives the bulk of its information about disorder, terrorism, and quasi-terrorism—and about official response to these law enforcement problems. What constitutes responsible selection of objectives and means for ongoing, nonemergency coverage is difficult to define with precision. But it is clear that a media policy that emphasizes reporting an emergency to the near exclusion of follow-up coverage constitutes a disservice to the public. Bearing in mind the interests and characteristics of its audience, every news organ should make a serious, complete, and noninflammatory presentation of information that will serve to put extraordinary violence in context, including:

1. Factual material documenting the aftermath of particular incidents, and emphasizing:
   a. Effects of extraordinary violence on individual victims and the community at large;
   b. Apprehension, trial, and sentencing of persons participating in extraordinary violence;
   c. Community reactions to law enforcement efforts in incident handling; and
   d. Official and nonofficial efforts to identify and address underlying grievances and precipitating social conditions.
2. Factual material not specifically tied to particular incidents, emphasizing such topics as:
   a. Local and national trends and tendencies in extraordinary violence;
   b. Available preventive security and law enforcement techniques applicable to extraordinary violence;
   c. Comparison of foreign and domestic experiences with extraordinary violence;
   d. Aims, characteristics, and records of terrorist groups;
   e. Background and recent history of quasi-terrorism and related forms of extraordinary violence; and
   f. Recent history and causative factors of mass disorder.
3. Editorial material analyzing options in public policy and private conduct, and where appropriate, recommending courses of action, in such topic areas as:
   a. Kinds and levels of preventive security;
   b. Law enforcement techniques;
   c. Community roles and responsibilities in emergencies; and
   d. Elimination of causes of extraordinary violence.

5 | "Media"

Combating Terrorism: Collection of Texts

European Conference of Ministers Responsible for Combating Terrorism, Council of Europe, Strasbourg, 1986

The mass media often have an important part to play in this kind of affair, either as an intermediary between the terrorists and those against whom they are trying to bring pressure to bear or as a means whereby the terrorists hope to gain publicity for what they are doing or for their ultimate goals, or again because the media are themselves the victims of extortion in that they are being compelled to publish—or not to publish—a prepared communiqué or other information.

Freedom of expression is a fundamental right in our democratic societies. Even the most serious crimes cannot justify restrictions other than those provided for in the Convention for the Protection of Human Rights and Fundamental Freedoms. It is mainly exercised through the mass media, whose decision-makers normally agree to abide voluntarily by the rules of professional ethics.

Any intervention by the public authorities might upset an often fragile equilibrium. For this reason the committee considers that in relations between the authorities and the media, even in cases as serious as those discussed in this report, any attempt to formalize relations or to bring them within a legal framework is likely to be damaging. Such relations must be established in a climate of trust, particularly during the period of crisis which occurs in such situations. Obviously, such a climate has to be fostered and permanently maintained so that benefit may be had from it as soon as a crisis breaks out.

Two limits on the freedom of the media should be pointed out here, however.

The first is that the media must not hamper or harm the authorities' actions. The hostage-taking at the Iranian embassy in London is a good example of that. While the security forces were preparing to storm the building to free the hostages, television cameras transmitted live pictures so that the terrorists inside the embassy had only to watch the transmission on their television screen to be fully informed about everything that was going on outside and were therefore in a position to prepare their response.

The second limit forbids the media to go further than the right to information demands—for example, by propagating views that the average reader would interpret as an apology for, or incitement to, criminal violence, cruel or inhuman acts, racial discrimination, or threats creating alarm in the public (such as threats of murder, looting, fire, etc.).

It has to be acknowledged that it is in certain instances difficult to draw a line between carrying out the duty to inform, on the one hand, and vindication, incitement, or even complicity, on the other. It appears that this line should be drawn both by the law and by professional ethics. But, it is better to rely in the first place on informal relations of mutual trust between the authorities and the media, based on well-established professional ethics, to ensure in each individual case that the mark is not overstepped.

It should be stressed too that the media can take positive steps in this connection. Thus in Italy, at the time of the kidnapping of Judge D'Urso by terrorists, most of the media not only refused to accede to the terrorists' request to publish certain statements, but on their own initiative also suspended the diffusion of any information about the affair.

6 | The Role of the Media

*The Report of the Senate (Canada) Special Committee on
Terrorism and the Public Safety, June 1987*

SUMMARY

Media coverage of terrorist incidents worldwide has been the subject of considerable comment and criticism. Much has been said about the relationship between terrorism and the media; little of that has been supported by objective, empirical analysis.

In Canada there is no evidence that media coverage before, during, or after a terrorist incident has, to date, cost lives or materially interfered with the resolution of an incident. The Committee, however, examined media coverage of several recent terrorist incidents in Canada and identified information broadcast during the incident that could have endangered lives or prejudiced the resolution of the incidents. The way in which the police related to the media also left much to be desired and, in one instance, the police themselves released information that could have endangered lives.

Some witnesses—including one media representative—urged the Committee to propose legislation to govern media coverage of terrorist incidents. The Committee rejected legislation at the outset. In the Committee's view, any intrusion on the freedom of the press can only be justified under circumstances akin to wartime conditions. . . . The Committee does not believe that the threat or incidence of terrorism in Canada presents or is likely soon to present such circumstances.

The Committee examined a number of guidelines or policies of national media organizations and outlets on covering terrorist incidents. In the main, these guidelines do not address some of the serious issues raised by recent media coverage of terrorist incidents in Canada and abroad. Perhaps because there have been relatively few terrorist incidents in Canada, some media people characterized the media and terrorism as a "non-issue" in Canada. The Press Councils abandoned an attempt to formulate guidelines, or to prepare a submission to the Committee. The Canadian Daily Newspaper Publishers' Association (CDNPA) said that the question of policies or guidelines was up to individual newspapers.

The Committee feels attention should be given to the role of the media in covering terrorist incidents, in particular to police-media relations during an incident and to better and more comprehensive guidelines. The Committee recommends that the federal government, through the Department of the

Solicitor General and the RCMP [Royal Canadian Mounted Police], initiate discussions with national media organizations to devise practical and effective guidelines. The Committee prepared an outline of such guidelines as a base on which to begin discussions.

BACKGROUND

The Committee noted the divergent views of journalists and others appearing before the Committee on both the current and the appropriate role of the media and an apparent lack of introspection in some quarters of the media on this subject. The Committee notes, in this regard, that media self-examination usually occurs after a widely publicized terrorist event and wanes shortly thereafter, perhaps to be resuscitated by a subsequent event. A wave of seminars, conferences, and guidelines was triggered by media coverage of a siege by Hanafi Muslims in Washington, D.C., by the TWA hijacking in Beirut, and in Canada, by the media's handling of the Toronto Transit Commission bombing threat and the Turkish embassy siege. With several notable exceptions, there has been little continuous discussion of performance, issues, and concerns among media, police, law, and government officials.

Much has been said or written about the media and terrorism. What has been said falls anywhere within a wide spectrum: At one extreme are those who contend the media coverage is "the oxygen of terrorism"; that there is a direct causal relationship between media coverage and terrorism and without media coverage, terrorism would wither and die. They point out that terrorist rarely obtain their demands or major concessions from governments. When judged on this basis, terrorism would represent a failure. Yet terrorism persists because it attracts media attention that, in turn, communicates the terrorists' causes and grievances to the world. At the other extreme are those who suggest that the media's impact on terrorism is positive. Without media coverage of terrorist threats and incidents, terrorists may be forced, they say, to devise increasingly horrendous atrocities in order to compel media and public attention.

It is important, at the outset, to note that certain types of terrorism, such as state-sponsored terrorism, usually avoid any coverage by or connections with the media. The activities of such terrorists are best conducted in a murky netherworld, far away from the light of media coverage and scrutiny. Other types of terrorism thrive on fear cultivated by rumor and panic. In such instances, accurate and objective media accounts may work against the terrorist by providing accuracy, proportion and perspective. Such terrorist groups also discourage media coverage of incidents.

There is evidence, however, that some relationship exists between media coverage and the types of terrorism that are principally of concern to Canada and to Canadians. The following section reviews some of the opinions expressed before the Committee by witnesses and in submissions.

A PRÉCIS OF TESTIMONY BEFORE THE COMMITTEE

The Potential Positive Impacts of the Media

THE FIRST CONTACT: Several witnesses stated that terrorists often trust the media, will contact journalists and try to bring the media into an incident. For example, in the Bahamian High Commission incident in Ottawa, in April 1986, the hostage-taker took with him a list of local television and radio stations and their telephone numbers. After establishing contact, he insisted that a reporter from a local television station act as an intermediary between him and the authorities. In the case of the Turkish embassy incident in Ottawa, the terrorists not only contacted local media outlets, but also tried to "negotiate with the media" to the exclusion of police and other authorities.

Since media people are often sought out and first contacted by terrorists, rather than being excluded from involvement in incidents, they suggest that there be more effective dialogue and consultation between media and the authorities so that the media knows better what to do or say when contacted by a terrorist. Certain responses by a journalist could go a long way toward defusing or stabilizing an incident. Other responses could inflame an incident and could endanger lives and property. Furthermore, both journalists and police often agree that the media can sometimes assist in the negotiation process.

Further, experience with previous terrorist incidents in Canada and abroad indicates, and several witnesses before the Committee confirmed, that the media will often be the first on the scene of a terrorist incident and it is impractical to try to exclude them. Furthermore, some witnesses pointed out the extent to which the police and government officials rely on media reports of a terrorist incident, both for information and alerting purposes. This is particularly true during the early stages of incidents and for those outside of Canada. In effect, the media can be a valuable early warning system for law enforcement and government organizations.

THE "SAFETY VALVE": Several witnesses pointed out that the primary objective of terrorists is to publicize propaganda, demands, or grievances, and violence or the threat of violence is often only a means to that end. Accordingly, terrorists will often settle for publicity, rather than actually committing the violence they threaten. Some witnesses and commentators on the subject also suggested that if media coverage were to be curtailed or prohibited, terrorists would perpetrate increasingly violent actions in order to compel coverage.

OBJECTIVE, FACTUAL REPORTING: Many journalists maintained that informed and accurate media coverage can help defuse a terrorist threat by reducing the spread of false and alarming rumors. They also held that media coverage can perform the invaluable role of informing the public on the extent and nature of a specific terrorist threat. In this way, the media may help reduce the level of "terror," thereby detracting from the effectiveness of terrorism. Although it was criticized by some witnesses, others felt that media coverage of the threatened bombing of the Toronto subway allowed people to make informed decisions on the level and validity of the threat and whether to use the subway.

FREEDOM OF THE PRESS: Several media witnesses referred to subsection 2(b) of the Canadian Charter of Rights and Freedoms, which guarantees "freedom of the press and other media" as a "fundamental freedom." Most witnesses strongly oppose any outside, especially government, interference in the way the press operates, or in whatever the press decides to publish. Some media representatives go as far as objecting to agreements or even consultations between the media and the authorities on the media's coverage of terrorist incidents. They fear that this could lead to management or co-optation of the media that would inhibit the healthy independent and critical position of the media with respect to the authorities.

The Potential Negative Impacts of Media Coverage

In the main, witnesses' criticism of the media's performance in reporting terrorism and terrorists' threats and incidents was directed at the electronic (television and radio) as opposed to the print media for any of the following reasons. The electronic media was said to be more continuous and have more immediacy. Television and radio can broadcast from the scene during an incident; the print media must await the next edition and have the opportunity to obtain background, provide perspective and balance. It was suggested that pictures and sound often portray the drama and excitement of an incident with more impact than print. Television cameras, lights, and tape recorders are sometimes more noticeable and perhaps obtrusive at a terrorist incident than a print reporter with a pen and notebook.

Witnesses suggested that it is the electronic media that usually break a story first. Testimony suggests that they are also compelled more to compress and summarize coverage in order to fit into relatively short time slots. This opens the electronic media to charges of news interpretation or management. Finally, witnesses stated that the electronic media are more readily accessible to the vast majority of Canadians and are more susceptible to the exigencies of competition. This does not mean that the print media generally escapes criticism for their behavior. It was pointed out that after the Turkish embassy incident, at least two Canadian newspapers urged in editorials that the Canadian government explore ways to have the "Armenian genocide" recognized, thus granting the terrorists a measure of success.

TERRORIST ACTS RELY ON MEDIA COVERAGE: This proposition heard by the Committee consists of two elements: The first is that the media plays an important—some said vital—role in communicating the threat and violence in order to engender terror. Media coverage, attracted by violence or the threat of violence, provides terrorist groups with a very cost-effective method of airing their grievances and objectives. The second element of this proposition is that media coverage of terrorist threats and incidents promotes" copycat terrorism." Some witnesses stated that coverage of a hijacking, for example, may plant the idea and the techniques of hijacking in the minds of those who have a grievance and may be inclined toward violence.

MEDIA COVERAGE PERSONALIZES A TERRORIST INCIDENT: During the hostage-taking incident at the Bahamian High Commission, there were repeated telephone interviews with and pictures taken of the hostage. The hijacking of TWA Flight 847 from Athens to Beirut and the hostages held by the Hizballah group in Lebanon provided ongoing opportunities for the media to interview hostages, friends, and relatives, or to broadcast messages from the hostages. Journalists stated that these "human interest angles" are an important element of media coverage.

Other witnesses pointed out, however, that while direct contact with hostages provides the media with an intimate and valuable perspective on what is happening during an incident, the consequences can be unfortunate. Several authorities on the subject point out that the publication of pictures, names, occupations, or addresses of hostages, families, and friends can subject them to threat or intimidation by the hostage-takers or their confederates, during or after the incident. During the Turkish embassy incident and in spite of requests to the contrary, the media televised pictures of diplomats and staff of the Turkish embassy. (Turkish diplomats in Ottawa and elsewhere apparently try to avoid being identified publicly, lest they be more easily targeted by terrorists.)

Commentators on the subject contend that in order to communicate terror to the citizenry, some terrorist incidents are most effective when they demonstrate the vulnerability of society to apparently random attack involving, whenever possible, innocent, everyday citizens. It is important then that terrorists personalize their attacks, that average citizens are seen to be at risk.

Further, police explained that in the resolution of a terrorist incident, such as a hijacking or a hostage-taking, governments and police usually avoid taking aggressive actions to force a quick end, unless the circumstances require them to do so. Negotiators will usually play for time, try to lower the sense of crisis and emergency and, thereby, achieve a peaceful solution without loss of life. They suggest that the personalization of an incident militates against this strategy. The natural reaction of citizens will usually be to sympathize with the hostages and question what the authorities are doing and why a resolution is taking so long. In this regard, some witnesses suggested media coverage may help present the terrorists as strong and the authorities as weak, bumbling, or disinterested.

PROVIDING INTELLIGENCE TO TERRORISTS: Witnesses stated that the media unintentionally sometimes provide invaluable intelligence to terrorists during an incident through broadcast news reports. Police contend that news about the total number of people in a building under siege could threaten those who have managed to hide. Information provided on hostages, families, and friends may also be dangerous. Terrorists have been known to select victims on the basis of race, religion, nationality, or even occupation. Such information can also be used to pressure hostages. Information provided by the press on Brigidier General Dozier, during his captivity by the Italian Red Brigades, is alleged to have been "the most valuable intelligence the Red Brigades were to secure."* Police pointed out that information provided through the media such as the location, movement, size, or plans of police assault teams, the location of police snipers or operations centers can endanger lives and prejudice an assault operation.

Police witnesses expressed frustration that broadcasters appear sometimes to lose sight of the fact that terrorists are usually capable of monitoring their coverage during an incident, either directly or through confederates.** In the heat of the moment and in a quest for facts to relate to their audiences, police fear that the media may disclose information that can endanger lives.

MEDIA BEHAVIOR CAN IMPEDE RESOLUTION OF A TERRORIST INCIDENT: During the Bahamian High Commission and Turkish embassy incidents in Ottawa, the hostage-takers received a number of calls from the media. These calls into the sites occupied the telephone lines and made it impossible for the police to establish continuous contact with the terrorists. Police eventually severed the telephone lines and established their own contact. In the view of the authorities involved, these calls by reporters into the sites impeded the resolution of the incidents.

Police point out that journalists may also unwittingly impact on the evolution of an incident. During the Turkish embassy incident, for example, a radio reporter contacted one of the terrorists and asked if he had any "short-term demands" other than a recognition of the Armenian genocide. According to police, the idea of "short-term" demands had not previously been raised and, from the reaction, had previously not been considered by the terrorists.

The Police Perspective

Testimony by police officers before the Committee made it clear that their basic approach is to handle a terrorist incident as quickly as possible and without loss of life. Relating to the media is, at best, a secondary consideration and, at worst, a major source of irritation.

In addition, police officers pointed out that in providing information to the media, they are trained to avoid anything that might prejudice the resolution of an incident, the fair trial of the alleged terrorists or might endanger the safety of victims or their families, either during or after the incident.

---

*Dr. Rudolf Levy, "Terrorism and the Media," *Military Intelligence*, p. 36.

**The example often referred to is an incident in Mogadishu, Somalia. On October 13, 1977, a Lufthansa 731 was hijacked and finally ended up in Mogadishu. To aid authorities, the pilot covertly provided information about the terrorists. When the media disclosed his activities, the pilot was killed by the terrorists.

With this in mind, most police officers find it best to "say nothing and brave the hostility of the press."

While some police officers have been trained in media relations, many have not, particularly for the tense, emergency environment of a terrorist incident. During the Turkish embassy siege, it was a police officer who disclosed to the press that the Turkish ambassador was lying just outside a window of the embassy, was injured, and could not be moved. This information, when relayed by the electronic media, put the ambassador's life at risk. The officer acknowledged that the mistake was made under the pressures of the moment and without realizing that TV cameras were broadcasting his comments live. (At the time of the incident, the officer handling media relations had not been trained in media relations, but has since completed courses at the Police College.)

COMMITTEE OBSERVATIONS AND RECOMMENDATIONS

A Review of Selected Terrorist Incidents

The Committee examined media coverage of the Turkish embassy siege and the Bahamian High Commission hostage-taking. While dramatic, compelling, and informative, the media released information during the incident that could have endangered lives, or could have interfered with police operations. (In both cases, televisions and/or radios were on and available to the terrorists.)

- In both cases, media representatives initiated and tried to maintain telephone contact with terrorists or hostages, blocking lines into the site.
- During the Turkish embassy incident, a radio reporter asked leading questions about "short-term demands" that had apparently not been made or even considered by the terrorists.
- In both cases, information was provided on the location or plans of police assault teams. In the Turkish embassy case, information was provided on the location of police snipers and the police operational headquarters that, in the words of one police officer, would have allowed the terrorists "to pick off our men like flies." During the Bahamian High Commission incident, a local radio reporter broadcasting from the scene disclosed that the Ottawa police SWAT team was moving into position in the offices immediately below the High Commission.
- In the Turkish embassy case, the media disclosed that the police intended to maneuver an armored vehicle into position to act as a barricade to rescue the injured ambassador.

Much of this information was obtained through observation or by monitoring police-band radio frequencies.

Police handling of these incidents also left much to be desired.

- In both cases, the police were slow to set up even basic facilities for briefing the press. In the Turkish incident, most of the briefings took the form of disorderly "scrums." The police officer dealing with the press was inadequately trained to perform the function.

- During the Turkish embassy incident, police officers briefing the press were apparently unaware of the technology available to television reporters, particularly the fact that interviews with the police were being broadcast instantaneously.

- During the Turkish embassy incident, police released to the media information on the location of the injured ambassador that put him at risk. During the Bahamian High Commission incident, the police refused to confirm or supply information to the media that was already in the public domain, or had been broadcast by other media outlets. This caused competitor stations to contact the High Commission direct, an action the police later criticized as irresponsible.

- During both incidents, the police were slow in cutting telephone lines into the sites and establishing their own contacts.

- During the Bahamian incident, a jurisdictional dispute between officers of the RCMP and the Ottawa Police Force did more to anger the hostage-taker and delay resolution than anything done by the media.

The Media

The Committee devised a set of questions relating to the media coverage of terrorist incidents. These questions were gleaned from existing policies and guidelines, from research, or from testimony of witnesses before the Committee. They would be the type of issues that would confront reporters covering a terrorist incident. The questions were posed to reporters, editors, and other media witnesses appearing before the Committee.

The Committee was intrigued that some of these questions were being considered for the first time, even by witnesses who had been actively engaged in the reporting of previous terrorist events in Canada or abroad. This might explain the wide variations in responses from witness to witness.

Several news organizations and media outlets have devised or are devising guidelines, policies, or procedures for the handling of terrorist incidents. After having reviewed media coverage of terrorist incidents in Canada and abroad and with the benefit of hindsight, the Committee has concluded that, in the main, the guidelines that are in force do not address some important issues that have been raised by media coverage of recent incidents. Even when guidelines exist, experience suggests that they are not always scrupulously followed. This is perhaps understandable in the Canadian context where there have been relatively few terrorist incidents and where, at least to date, the media has had no measurable impact on them.

QUESTIONS

- ■ Would you respect a police perimeter at a terrorist incident?
- ☐ Would you try to get a vantage point outside the perimeter to see and report what was happening inside the perimeter?
- ☐ Would your presence at the incident be unobtrusive, or would it be obvious "the media was there"?
- ☐ Would you report the maneuvering of a SWAT Team getting ready to assault the building?

- ■ Would you initiate interviews with relatives/friends of hostages during a hostage incident?
- ☐ Would you report the names of hostages?
- ☐ Would you report the status of hostages (e.g. alive, dead, frightened, hungry, angry, etc.)?

- ■ If information concerning a terrorist incident came to you, would you release it if the authorities asked you not to?
- ☐ If police said the information could endanger lives?
- ☐ If police said the information could prejudice an assault operation?
- ☐ If police said the information could frustrate negotiations or delay resolution of the incident?
- ☐ If police said the information could cause "pain and suffering" to families and friends of the hostages?

- ■ Would you try to contact, by telephone or otherwise, terrorists or hostages during a terrorist incident?

- ■ Would you immediately contact police, before or after public release?
- ☐ If a terrorist contacts you immediately after initiating a terrorist incident?
- ☐ If you became aware of a terrorist incident to occur in a few days or immediately?
- ☐ If you were the recipient of a communiqué, demands, propaganda, etc., from a terrorist?

- ■ Would you place yourself or allow yourself to be placed in a position of negotiating with terrorists?

- ■ Would you consent to a live interview with a terrorist?
- ☐ During an incident?
- ☐ After an incident?

- ■ Would you publish demands or propaganda of a terrorist group?
- ☐ During an incident or after?
- ☐ In full, edited or summary form?
- ☐ If police asked you not to?
- ☐ If police asked you to?

MEDIA RESTRAINT: Testimony before the Committee clearly indicates that effective guidelines raise serious issues and concerns with many media people. First, media guidelines prepared or imposed by someone other than the media themselves could expect stiff opposition from most journalists. Second, in view of the relatively few terrorist incidents that have occurred in Canada and the lack of any evidence that the media have had an impact on them one way or the other, journalists question the need for guidelines at all. Third, how can guidelines foresee every eventuality in future terrorist incidents in which the media, intentionally or unintentionally, might have an impact? Finally, media witnesses expressed concern that any significant degree of restraint in withholding information relating to a terrorist incident, regardless of the reasons, could damage the media's credibility and their perceived objectivity and neutrality. As one witness stated, "The public would say: If they (the media) are not publishing this for whatever reason, what else are they holding back?"

Testimony before the Committee indicated clearly that media coverage and police actions during at least two terrorist incidents in Canada could very easily have endangered lives or prejudiced resolution of the incidents. Effective guidelines could well have helped the journalists and police involved avoid some of the pitfalls. The Committee also notes that the media have guidelines in other areas such as the coverage of natural disasters or civil disorders. With relatively minor modifications, these guidelines could be adapted to terrorist situations. Finally, the Committee notes that the media has engaged and continues to engage in some restraint in reporting on terrorist and other incidents. The names of traffic accident victims are not usually disclosed until next of kin have been notified. During the TWA 847 hijacking, the international media knew, but did not report, that a member of the National Security Agency was on board the aircraft. There are other examples of media restraint in Canada, some of which will be discussed below.

One of the most difficult questions facing the Committee was whether media restraint would result in terrorists resorting to increasingly horrendous atrocities to compel media coverage. The Committee believes that there are limits to the violence terrorists can mount, either because of resources and capabilities, or because of the impact increasing violence would have on the terrorists' ability to achieve their aims. Ian Smart points out that the terrorist

> can seldom afford to push his wider popular audience beyond the limits of terror and pity into a mood of outraged revulsion. . . . He fails if his actions and their effects are so repellant that his audience . . . becomes intent on abetting the government in an effort to eradicate terrorism at any cost. And he fails most disastrously when revulsion reaches his natural supporters or the mass of the community in whose interests he claims to act.*

*Ian Smart, "International Terrorism," in *Behind the Headlines* 44 no. 3 (February 1987): 10.

The Police

The Committee agrees with the testimony of many media witnesses that police-media relations are generally poorly organized, fraught with mutual suspicion sometimes bordering on antagonism, as well as a lack of sympathy or understanding by the police of the media's role and functions. The media hold that this situation results in much of the behavior for which the media is subsequently criticized. Journalists argue that the general police attitude during or after a terrorist incident is to tell the media as little as possible and sometimes even to engage in "disinformation."

Some journalists alleged that police often provide information to "preferred" journalists and not to others. This, in turn, leads to hostility, resentment, and competition between news organizations that can lead to irresponsible behavior, as illustrated by some of the incidents already reviewed in this part. Some members of the media also contend that the police's aversion to media coverage is motivated, not only by the police's desire to conduct operations unimpeded, but also because media coverage encourages or imposes increased accountability to the public for the police's conduct of the operations.

In reviewing some recent terrorist and criminal incidents, the Committee identified some obvious flaws in the way in which the police related to the media: Often the police officer responsible for media relations was relatively junior and did not have the requisite authority or expertise to decide which information could be released to the press and what could not. Adequate facilities were not always available for press briefings. The police media relations officer was not always adequately trained for the function.

The Committee noted with particular concern that much of the criticism of poor media relations was directed at the RCMP, not at provincial or municipal police forces. The Committee also noted that, to date, the RCMP does not have a media relations capability expressly designed to conduct media relations during a terrorist incident in which it is involved. As a consequence of testimony before the Committee, including some from the RCMP, the Committee feels it important that the RCMP fundamentally rethink how it communicates with the public and relates with the press and, in particular, establish an effective media relations capability to deal with the press during a terrorist incident in which the RCMP is involved.

There have been several criminal incidents in Canada—usually involving hostages—where the media refrained from publishing information at the request of the police, on the grounds that its publication could endanger lives or interfere with the resolution of the incident. Based on these precedents and on experience in other countries, in particular the United Kingdom,*

---

*The London Metropolitan Police Force follows the "Mark's Guidelines" for media relations that are essentially identical to the approach recommended in this part. The guidelines were named after Sir Robert Mark, who issued the guidelines during his tenure as chief commissioner. During the kidnapping of German industrialist Hans Martin Schleyer, the German government successfully obtained agreement from the media to restrain its coverage until the incident was terminated. In return, the media were given a detailed account of developments as they occurred, by the authorities. With the exception of a few minor publications, the German media respected the agreement.

several witnesses suggested that substantial gains can be made in this direction.

Several witnesses felt it appropriate and often necessary that information be withheld from public release during an incident, but that the same information need not be withheld from journalists for release later on. They had in mind a procedure whereby journalists would be fully and continuously briefed by police officers on all aspects of the situation, including the police's plan for resolution. In addition, cameramen and still photographers would be allowed safe access to take pictures for public release later on. Suggestions were made by witnesses that the media could be briefed on a pool basis, whereby a few journalists would be briefed by police and these journalists would, in turn, provide the information to the remaining journalists, on the basis of strict equality. In briefing the journalists, however, the police would clearly identify the information that could be released to the public immediately and the information that could not be released until the incident is over. The grounds for not releasing certain information would be that to do so would endanger life, or interfere with the resolution of the incident. This approach would result in the media knowing all during an incident, but being allowed to publish or broadcast certain information only after the incident is over, or sooner with police authorization. The condition would be not only that the media respect the police's directions on the release of such information, but also that the media refrain from using other sources of information, such as telephone calls to the terrorists that could interfere with police handling of the incident.

Some witnesses recommended another innovation for major urban centers: As a matter of police policy, any journalist accepted into the "pool" could be accredited by the police. Police accreditation could include "auditing" or participation in at least some police antiterrorist training programs. It was argued that this would raise the journalists' credibility with the police and would help the journalists evaluate and understand the police actions during an incident, in particular the necessity to withhold certain information temporarily.

Police officers are less than enthusiastic about this approach. While there are occasions on which such an approach has worked,* there are also occasions in which it has failed.** Police are concerned that one inexperienced or dramatically inclined broadcaster could prejudice the entire approach. Police are also concerned that the competitive nature of the broadcasting industry will induce breaches. Police point out that several national news

---

*For example, in January 1978 a hostage-taking incident began in Calgary and ended in Oak Lake. Certain information came into the hands of the media that, in the opinion of the police, could have made resolution of the incident more difficult. At the request of the police, the media refrained from relaying this information until the incident was completed.

**For example, during the kidnapping of Edmonton businessman Peter Pocklington, a local television station shot some film footage. The police thought the broadcast of this tape could detract from their attempts to resolve the incident quickly and peacefully. Another television station broadcast the footage and the original station then felt compelled to follow suit.

organizations refuse, as a matter of policy, to respect embargos on announcements and would likely extend that policy to information provided during a terrorist incident. Finally, police are concerned that the agreement might well be respected by the media within a defined geographic area, but would break down as soon as journalists from outside the area arrive who were unaware of or refused to respect the agreement.

After careful consideration of the evidence and testimony placed before it, the Committee finds the police's concerns valid and compelling. While recognizing that such arrangements have sometimes worked and are being discussed by the police and media in several cities as a model for handling future incidents, the Committee has no confidence that this approach can be expected to work generally, or even frequently.

GUIDELINES FOR MEDIA AND POLICE

Media

In light of the conclusions set out above, the Committee is drawn to guidelines prepared by the media, in consultation with government and law enforcement officials, and monitored and reviewed by the media's own professional associations. In the Committee's view, there should be two basic principles underlying the preparation of such guidelines. First, the media's coverage of a terrorist incident should not endanger lives or property or interfere with the authorities in their attempts to resolve the incident by force, negotiation, or otherwise.*** Second, while guidelines will suggest the media restrict itself from broadcasting information during a terrorist incident, there should be no limitation on the media's ability to release information after the incident, as long as doing so would not endanger lives of former hostages, their families or friends, or prejudice future assault operations by SWAT teams.

In order to assist in discussions and to provide a starting point for a set of guidelines, the Committee has devised the following outline, which addresses gaps the Committee feels exist in current guidelines or policies.

LIVE COVERAGE: Through live coverage of a terrorist incident, the media may unwittingly and unintentionally provide information which is of assistance to the terrorists, which endangers lives or jeopardizes or delays the resolution of the incident. Accordingly, an integral part of any guidelines should be to address the live and unedited coverage of terrorist incidents.

CONTACT WITH TERRORISTS: When journalists call into the site of a terrorist incident or undertake interviews with terrorists over the telephone or

***This principle may appear to be trite. The Committee noted, however, comments made by senior journalists before the Committee and elsewhere that indicate this principle is not universally accepted in the media. See for example, comments attributed to or made by journalists in Arthur Lewis, "Press and Police Clash over Hostage-Takings," *Bulletin*, Centre for Investigative Journalism, Ottawa, March 1986; and Public Broadcasting System Series on "Terrorism and the Media," January–February 1987.

otherwise, they run the risk of overloading telephone lines into the site and making it more difficult for the police to establish and maintain contact with the terrorist. Furthermore, direct contact with and coverage of a terrorist feeds his ego, strengthens his cause among potential supporters, and may prolong the crisis. Accordingly, media guidelines should caution journalists on initiating contact with terrorists, suggest ways in which journalists can involve the police in discussions with the terrorists, and encourage the journalists to refer calls from terrorists to the senior journalist on duty at the time. The police can assist the media by advising reporters on how to handle such calls, the type of information journalists should try to obtain to help defuse or resolve the incident, what to say and what not to say.

MEDIA AS INTERMEDIARIES: Negotiation with terrorists is both an art and a science for which selected police officers are intensively trained and experienced. An inexperienced negotiator may exacerbate the crisis. The media's guidelines should caution members of the press on the serious potential repercussions of injecting themselves into such negotiations.

POLICE PERIMETERS: During a terrorist incident, police will be preoccupied with the handling of the incident and should not be distracted by members of the public and the media trying to intrude onto the site. Further, when terrorists catch sight of lights, cameras, and microphones, it can interfere with police attempts to diffuse the incident and bring it to a quick solution without injury or loss of life. Accordingly, the media guidelines should encourage the media to respect police perimeters and to make their presence at or close to the site as unobtrusive as possible.

PREPARATIONS: Media coverage during a terrorist incident can provide valuable information to the terrorists, either directly or through their confederates on the outside. Terrorists are usually able to monitor radio and television broadcasts during an incident. Accordingly, media guidelines should caution journalists on broadcasting information during the incident that could endanger lives, prolong the incident or jeopardize an assault operation, such as the presence, on site, of police assault teams, the location of police snipers, observation or command posts, or police plans or maneuvers to position or undertake an assault and rescue operation.

PROPAGANDA: The essential purpose of a terrorist act is to publish (and hopefully to gain sympathy or support for) the terrorists' aims, objectives, or grievances. When the media reports terrorist propaganda, especially in unedited form or without comment, it may play into the terrorists' hands and help make terrorism viable. Accordingly, media guidelines should give guidance on how and when to broadcast or report terrorist propaganda or terrorists' demands.

HOSTAGES: Providing information on hostages during an incident can give terrorists valuable information that they can use to further their objectives or to intimidate or pressure hostages. Accordingly, media guidelines should caution journalists on the release of the names, number, and status of hostages during an incident.

IDENTIFICATION OF TERRORISTS: The media is able to confer status on terrorists or the groups they claim to represent merely by mentioning their names. Accordingly, media guidelines could address the issue of how to refer to terrorists, perhaps encouraging journalists to refer to them generically as "gunmen". . . . Furthermore, spokespersons for ethnic groups made strong representations to the Committee about the harm done to their communities by being implicated through association of racial or religious origin with those very few who carry out terrorist attacks. Given the speed and surprise factor associated with terrorist incidents, this is clearly a difficult area of concern that deserves consultation between representatives of ethnic communities, on one hand, and the police and the media on the other.

AFTER THE INCIDENT: The guidelines should caution journalists about the publication or broadcasting of information after a terrorist incident that could reasonably be expected to prejudice the resolution of subsequent terrorist incidents, or endanger released hostages. Given the potential sensitivity of such information, the media may be requested to withhold the names of members of the police assault teams, their permanent headquarters or special techniques. Further, it may be advisable under certain circumstances to withhold the names and addresses of hostages, lest they be put at risk or intimidated by confederates of the hostage-takers.

Police

PERIMETERS: The police should move as quickly as possible to secure a cordon around the site of a terrorist incident and secure the area. In light of past experience, police will have to consider establishing perimeters that neutralize the ability of the electronic media to use telephoto lenses and other technology to broadcast developments in or close to the site during the incident. This will usually involve moving reporters and members of the public far away from the area. Telephone lines into the site should be cut immediately and the police should devise, in advance, more effective ways of establishing communication links with terrorists and hostages at a terrorist incident.

BRIEFING ROOMS: As soon as possible after an incident begins, police should establish a location close to the site, but outside the perimeter, where police officers will be available to brief the media. In view of past experience, whenever possible police should avoid "media scrums" to brief the press.

POLICE MEDIA RELATIONS OFFICER: The effectiveness of police-media relations during an incident will depend to a considerable extent on the police quickly designating a senior police officer with good communications skills, media relations training and the knowledge of what is going on at the incident to deal with the media. Whenever possible, this officer should be of requisite seniority to speak with the authority of the commanding officer at the site and, thereby, be able to designate information that can be released to the press and to identify any information that cannot, at least for the time being, be released to the public on the grounds that it could endanger life or prejudice the resolution of the incident.

AFTER THE INCIDENT: The police should consider ways to provide the media with extensive post-incident briefings and, during the incident, explore with the media ways to give the media opportunities safely to take pictures of the site for release after the incident is over.

Conclusions

The Committee is under no illusion that implementation of even the most comprehensive guidelines will reduce the number or severity of terrorist incidents in Canada, nor is the Committee under any illusion that guidelines will be religiously or universally respected. The existence of effective guidelines may, however, save a life or speed the resolution of a terrorist incident.

In the final analysis, however, when a terrorist incident occurs, the paramount consideration must be the resolution of the incident in such a way as to minimize danger to life or property. The primary responsibility for this lies with police officers. The Committee has concluded that to resolve a terrorist incident, law enforcement officers are not only permitted, but indeed have the obligation, to take and enforce whatever steps they deem necessary within the law to secure the situation as quickly as possible. The most practical and effective way to minimize media intrusion or inadvertence is for police to take immediate action to restrict the media's physical access to the scene. After the incident, the media will have an opportunity to appraise the methods by which police handled the incident.

Police must realize, however, that the media do form an integral part of any police strategy to handle a terrorist incident. As indicated earlier in this part by witnesses, terrorists may settle for publicity through the media rather than perpetrate the violence they threaten; strategic release of terrorist propaganda or demands by authorities through the media might assist in negotiations; while the release of some information during an incident could endanger lives or jeopardize negotiations or an assault operation. Accordingly, the Committee strongly recommends that the federal government, through the Department of the Solicitor General and the RCMP, initiate discussions with representatives of national media organizations and outlets as well as selected provincial and municipal police forces to design practical guidelines. The Committee would like to see a process developed whereby police and media groups in an ever-growing number of centers reach agreements that are consistent and would eventually merge into national guidelines.

In the Committee's view it is imperative that these discussions occur soon, prior to a terrorist incident that results in problems that could have been avoided through implementation of such guidelines.

7 | The Role of the Media

Report of the International Task Force on Prevention of Nuclear Terrorism, June 1986

ROLE OF THE MEDIA

To avoid panic as the result of premature or inaccurate information during a nuclear terrorist emergency, guidelines should be established now among media and government representatives on disseminating information in such a crisis.

1. Because of the possibility of widespread panic, injury, and death resulting from a credible threat by nuclear terrorists, government officials and media representatives should cooperate in planning how to provide timely and accurate information in such a contingency.

2. To the extent possible, joint guidelines should be developed in anticipation of a crisis by the responsible national government agencies with regard to how and when information will be disseminated during a crisis. The key consideration should be at what point in a crisis, if the threat proves real, there still would be time to order an evacuation in a manner that minimizes injury and death and promotes public order. Leading media representatives and state and local officials should be invited to participate in preparation of the guidelines.

BACKGROUND

In covering terrorist incidents, the media is presented with some very complex challenges: they must be responsible, which may mean withholding information; they must avoid being manipulated, which may mean declining to cover an event that would normally be considered newsworthy, and, sometimes when lives are at stake, they must subjugate the competitive urge to be first with the news.

There are recent examples of these challenges. In some cases, the media have withheld information. For example, during the American embassy crisis in Iran, some American reporters learned that six Americans known to have been in the embassy were not being held by the Iranians. The reporters further learned that those men had escaped to another embassy, which they understood to be the Canadian embassy. This had actually happened, but the information was not published until after the hostages had left Iran. Again during last year's hijacking of TWA Flight 847 with 153 hostages aboard, reporters covering the incident learned, but did not report, that one of the hostages was a member of the U.S. National Security Agency.

In other cases, the media has allowed the intense heat of competition to rule its behavior. The coverage of the TWA hijacking became a scramble by the U.S. television networks, to be first with an interview with the hijackers. The networks ran promotion campaigns on the air and in American newspapers boasting about their scoops. Again, in 1983 sixty people were killed in a bomb attack on the U.S. embassy in Beirut. Reporters discovered that the U.S. had managed to intercept coded communications between Syria and Iran during the period of the bombing, and one television network and a newspaper columnist reported this fact. The coded communications stopped.

British Prime Minister Margaret Thatcher has encouraged the news media to restrict their coverage of terrorist actions. She has said that the media must find ways of starving the terrorist and the hijacker of what she termed the oxygen of publicity on which they depend. However, media executives in Britain, and in America, have indicated they have no intention of following Mrs. Thatcher's request. Given the increasing daring of terrorist groups and the greater lethal potential of their acts, the prospect of nuclear terrorism raises a host of new considerations with ever more serious consequences. It is one thing for the media to attempt responsible and informative coverage of the kidnapping of an American general in Italy or the holding hostage of an airplane, but the coverage of a terrorist event where a nuclear device has just exploded, or where a terrorist group is threatening to explode such a device, may call for extraordinary, and hitherto unwarranted, cooperation between the media and local and central government.

Although journalists have a healthy bias against such cooperation, the media has indeed cooperated voluntarily on occasion. In Britain, the government has successfully censored information by application of a self-denying ordinance with no legal force, known as the D-Notice, by which editors, represented by a committee, agree not to mention or discuss a topic said by the government to be of importance to national security. But a nuclear terrorist incident could involve a situation where the media become an integral part of saving lives—for example, in the evacuation of towns or cities affected, or in trying to prevent panic. The success of such operations could depend on the timely disclosure of carefully selected information.

Media executives recognize that a greater degree of cooperation between the media and government might be required in certain special circumstances. And most of the media appears willing to explore ways in which their responsibilities can be carried out in concert with government. But this willingness requires reinforcement, and there currently are no continuous, formalized lines of communication on how this cooperation would work in extraordinary cases like nuclear terrorism.

In anticipation of such a crisis, government officials could conduct mock exercises with media participation, as well as prepare background materials and conduct background briefings on weapons effects, reactor accidents and other possible outcomes of nuclear terrorism. In this way, the media could become better informed, and misinformation and panic could be minimized during an actual crisis.

APPENDIX C

Selected Media Guidelines*

*Reprinted by permission.

8 | CBS News Standards

Because the facts and circumstances of each case vary, there can be no specific self-executing rules for the handling of terrorist/hostage stories. CBS News will continue to apply the normal tests of news judgment and if, as so often they are, these stories are newsworthy, we must continue to give them coverage despite the dangers of "contagion." The disadvantages of suppression are, among other things, (1) adversely affecting our credibility ("What else are the news people keeping from us?"); (2) giving free rein to sensationalized and erroneous word-of-mouth rumors; and (3) distorting our news judgments for some extraneous judgmental purpose. These disadvantages compel us to continue to provide coverage.

Nevertheless, in providing for such coverage there must be thoughtful, conscientious care and restraint. Obviously, the story should not be sensationalized beyond the actual fact of its being sensational. We should exercise particular care in how we treat the terrorist/kidnapper.

More specifically:

1. An essential component of the story is the demands of the terrorist/ kidnapper and we must report those demands. But we should avoid providing an excessive platform for the terrorist/kidnapper. Thus, unless such demands are succinctly stated and free of rhetoric and propaganda, it may be better to paraphrase the demands instead of presenting them directly through the voice or picture of the terrorist/ kidnapper.

2. Except in the most compelling circumstances, and then only with the approval of the President of CBS News, or in his absence, the Senior Vice President of News, there should be no live coverage of the terrorist/kidnapper since we may fall into the trap of providing an unedited platform for him. (This does not limit live on-the-spot reporting by CBS News reporters, but care should be exercised to assure restraint and context.)

3. News personnel should be mindful of the probable need by the authorities who are dealing with the terrorist for communication by telephone and hence should endeavor to ascertain, wherever feasible, whether our own use of such lines would be likely to interfere with the authorities' communications.

4. Responsible CBS News representatives should endeavor to contact experts dealing with the hostage situation to determine whether they have any guidance on such questions as phraseology to be avoided, what kinds of questions or reports might tend to exacerbate the situation, etc. Any such recommendations by established authorities on the

scene should be carefully considered as guidance (but not as instruction) by CBS News personnel.

5. Local authorities should also be given the name or names of CBS personnel whom they can contact should they have further guidance or wish to deal with such delicate questions as a newsman's call to the terrorists or other matters which might interfere with authorities dealing with the terrorists.

6. Guidelines affecting our coverage of civil disturbances are also applicable here, especially those which relate to avoiding the use of inflammatory catchwords or phrases, the reporting of rumors, etc. As in the case of policy dealing with civil disturbances, in dealing with a hostage story reporters should obey all police instructions but report immediately to their superiors any such instructions that seem to be intended to manage or suppress the news.

7. Coverage of this kind of story should be in such overall balance as to length that it does not unduly crowd out other important news of the hour/day.

9 | The *Courier-Journal* and the *Louisville Times*

The following are guidelines for the newspapers' coverage in the event terrorists take and hold hostages in our area.

It will be our policy to cover the story fully and accurately. To do otherwise—to withhold information—could destroy our credibility and give life to reckless and exaggerated rumors in the community.

At the same time, our approach will be one of care and restraint. We will avoid sensationalism in what we write and how we display it, taking care not to play the story beyond its real significance.

We will make every effort not to become participants in the event. We will resist being used by the terrorists to provide a platform for their propaganda.

If terrorists demand that we publish specific information, we will agree to do so only if we are convinced that not to publish it would further endanger the life of a hostage. Our decision on whether to publish will be made only after consultation with the most senior editor available and, when possible, top police officials.

We will always be mindful of the dangers in telephoning terrorists or hostages for interviews during the event, realizing that such action could interrupt vital negotiations or incite the terrorists to violence.

We will assign experienced staff members to the story. We will involve the papers' top news officials when making decisions.

Insofar as possible, we will maintain contact with the responsible law enforcement officials dealing with the situation. It will always be our aim to avoid taking any action that would interfere with the proper execution of duties by police or other officials.

Although we cannot be responsible for the coverage by other news media, we can and will conduct a constant review of our own performance.

10 | The *Sun-Times* and *Daily News* Standards for Coverage of Terrorism

Recognizing that circumstances vary in each story, the following standards are meant for general guidance.

1. Normal tests of news judgment will determine what to publish despite the dangers of contagion, since the adverse effects of suppression are greater.

2. Coverage should be thoughtful and restrained and not sensationalized beyond the innate sensation of the story itself. Inflammatory catchwords, phrases, and rumors should be avoided.

3. Demands of terrorists and kidnappers should be reported as an essential point of the story but paraphrased when necessary to avoid unbridled propaganda.

4. Reporters should avoid actions that would further jeopardize the lives of hostages or police.

5. Reporters should obey all police instructions but report immediately to their supervisors any such instructions that seem to manage or suppress the news.

6. Supervising editors and reporters should contact authorities to seek guidance—not instructions—on the use of telephones or other facilities, the reporting of negotiations or police strategies.

7. Editors, reporters, and photographers should not become part of the story, should not participate in negotiations and should not ask terrorists about deadlines.

8. The senior supervisory editor should determine what—if any—information should be withheld or deferred after consultation with reporters and appropriate authorities.

9. The constant objective should be to provide a credible report without hampering authorities or endangering life.

11 | Guidelines of United Press International

Genuine concern has been expressed by the news media. There is concern that spectacles such as the Hanafi siege in Washington may turn into media events. There is concern that the media are being used as a forum by terrorists and kidnappers to express their views. There is concern about the definition, degree, and perspective of the news media coverage.

Most editors agree that these happenings must be reported. Editorials have pointed to the Constitution, the credibility of a free press, and the public's right to know.

Then where do we draw the line between legitimate news coverage and being exploited? The answer seems to be in individual news judgment and sense of responsibility.

There can be no clearly defined policy for terrorist and kidnapping stories. The circumstances vary in each case. UPI has established a set of guidelines that we feel are workable in most circumstances.

- We will judge each story on its own, and if a story is newsworthy we will cover it despite the dangers of contagion.
- Our coverage will be thoughtful, conscientious, and show restraint.
- We will not sensationalize a story beyond the fact of it being sensational.
- We will report the demands of terrorists and kidnappers as an essential point of the story but not provide an excessive platform for their demands.
- We will do nothing to jeopardize lives.
- We will not become a part of the story.
- If we do talk to a kidnapper or terrorist, we will not become a part of the negotiations.
- If there has been no mention of a deadline, we will not ask the kidnapper or terrorist if there is one.
- In all cases we will apply the rule of common sense.

ABOUT THE EDITORS AND
CONTRIBUTORS

Yonah Alexander is professor of international studies and director of the Institute for Studies in International Terrorism at the State University of New York; a research professor at the Elliott School of International Affairs at the George Washington University, and a Senior Fellow at the U.S. Global Strategy Council in Washington, D.C. He serves as editor in chief of *Terrorism: An International Journal,* and *Political Communication and Persuasion: An International Journal.* He also serves as series editor for books on terrorism by Martinus Nijhoff, Brassey's (US), Inc., and University Microfilm International. Professor Alexander has published over forty books on terrorism and international affairs.

Richard Latter serves as associate director of Wilton Park, where he has been a member of the academic staff since 1987. He studied political theory and institutions at Liverpool University, and international relations at the London School of Economics. From 1977 through 1987, he served as assistant to the director, and subsequently as deputy-director, of the International Statistical Institute, The Hague, the Netherlands. From 1984 through 1987, he was a lecturer at Webster University in Leiden, the Netherlands. In addition to terrorism, his current topics of interest include security questions, alliance politics, and arms control. Mr. Latter's writings include *The Making of American Foreign Policy in the Middle East, 1945–1948,* from Garland Publishing (1986).

The Right Honorable Lord Chalfont, OBE, MC, PC, served for twenty-two years in the British army, during which time he took part in counterterrorist operations in Cyprus, Malaya, and the Middle East, both as an intelligence officer and as an infantry commander. When he left the army in 1961, he became defense correspondent of *The Times* of London and in 1964 was appointed minister of state at the Foreign and Commonwealth Office.

In 1979 Lord Chalfont took part in the conference on international terrorism in Jerusalem organized by the Jonathan Institute; and in 1984 he was chairman of the second Jonathan Institute Conference on International Terrorism in Washington, D.C. In 1986 Lord Chalfont became chairman of the Institute for the Study of Terrorism.

He has published *The Sword and the Spirit,* an analysis of American military power; *Waterloo: The Story of Three Armies;* a biography of Lord Montgomery of Alamein; and a study of the American Strategic Defense Initiative entitled *Star Wars–Suicide or Survival?* His latest work, *Defence of The Realm,* an analysis of British defense policy, was published by Collins in November.

Lord Chalfont is chairman of the All Party Defence Group in the House of Lords.

Søren Elmquist is the head of the Danish Broadcasting Corporation's News and Current Affairs Department. As such, he is responsible for the only nationwide radio news network in Denmark. He is also responsible for putting into practice the parliamentary requirements on the broadcasting of alarm messages and national crisis information. He is therefore a member of the Danish Public Crisis Management Committee.

Educated at the University of Copenhagen, studying law and political science, Mr. Elmquist started his journalistic career as a politicoscientific commentator on the weekly newspaper *Weekendavisen Berlingske Aften.* He joined the Danish Broadcasting Corporation in 1974, starting as editor of political affairs and advancing to chief subeditor and assistant head of department. In 1985 he was appointed head of department.

He has studied crisis information and management in a number of European countries and in the United States and has lectured on the subject in various countries.

John E. Finn is an assistant professor at Wesleyan University, Middletown, Connecticut. Educated at Princeton University and Georgetown University Law School, Professor Finn has written a book on antiterrorist legislation in Western Europe and is an expert on the U.S. First Amendment as it affects media reporting of national security issues.

Sir John Hermon was a police officer for thirty-eight years and chief constable of the Royal Ulster Constabulary for nine years. Before his retirement in 1989, he commanded a force of more than 12,500 men and women (regular and reserve), with the army operating in support of the police.

In addition to the many responsibilities Sir John discharged in various ranks with the RUC during twenty years of terrorism in Northern Ireland, he has contributed to national and international understanding of conflict by traveling and lecturing nationally and internationally.

His services were recognized by Her Majesty with the award of a knighthood in 1982. He is also a commander/brother of the Order of St. John.

Alan Protheroe is chairman of the Association of British Editors, a member of the Council of RUSI (Royal United Services Institute for Defence Studies), a director of Visnews, and managing director of SSVC (Services Sound and Vision Corporation).

Mr. Protheroe was born in 1934 at St. David's Pembrokeshire and was educated at Maesteg Grammar School, Glamorgan. After three years as a reporter and subeditor on the *Glamorgan Gazette,* he carried out his national service with the Welsh Regiment.

He joined the BBC in 1957 as a contract reporter for BBC Wales. In 1960 he was appointed industrial correspondent for Wales, and in 1963 he became news editor for Wales. In 1969 he was redesignated editor for Wales (news and current affairs). He moved to London in 1970 to be assistant editor for television news. He was appointed editor of television news in 1977 and became assistant director for news and current affairs in 1980.

Mr. Protheroe was appointed assistant director general of the BBC in 1982, a post which he held until 1987. He was responsible for the standards of the BBC's journalism, exercising, on the director general's behalf, the day-to-day responsibilities of editor in chief across the entire spectrum of the BBC's immense radio and television news and public affairs programming.

In 1980 Mr. Protheroe was appointed a member of the Order of the British Empire (Military Division) for services to the U.K. Reserve Army. He also holds the territorial decoration and serves as a colonel (late Royal Regiment of Wales) at the Ministry of Defence.

Born in 1944, *Barry Rosen* was educated at the City University of New York, the Maxwell School of Public Policy at Syracuse University, and Columbia.

Mr. Rosen taught in Teheran as a Peace Corps volunteer from 1968 to 1970. He was chief of Central Asian broadcasts for the Voice of America (VOA) before becoming press attaché at the U.S. embassy in Teheran in November 1978. While serving in this capacity, he was taken hostage in 1979. After his release, he was seconded by the State Department to Columbia University, left the Foreign Service, and became assistant to the president of Brooklyn College, City University of New York.

Mr. Rosen was twice awarded the State Department's award for valor. He speaks widely on the subject of terrorism, has edited or written three books, writes for the *Los Angeles Times,* and has appeared on all four major U.S. television networks.

Paul Wilkinson holds the chair in International Relations at the University of St. Andrews. He previously held the same position at Aberdeen University and was head of the Department of Politics and International Relations there.

Professor Wilkinson's best-known books include *Terrorism and the Liberal State* (rev. ed., 1986) and *The New Fascists* (rev. ed., 1983). He is joint editor and contributor to *Contemporary Research on Terrorism* (1987), associate editor of *Terrorism: An International Journal,* and chairman of the Research Foundation for the Study of Terrorism. He is series editor of Key Concepts in International Relations, published by Allen and Unwin. Since 1986 he has been special consultant on terrorism to CBS (America) and ITN (London).